A 21st Century Memoir

JOSEPH H. HAFKENSCHIEL JR. MD

iUniverse, Inc.
New York   Bloomington

A 21st Century Memoir

iUniverse books may be ordered through booksellers or by contacting:

iUniverse
1663 Liberty Drive
Bloomington, IN 47403
www.iuniverse.com
1-800-Authors (1-800-288-4677)

ISBN: 978-1-4401-1560-8 (sc)
ISBN: 978-1-4401-1562-2 (hc)
ISBN: 978-1-4401-1561-5 (ebook)

Printed in the United States of America

iUniverse rev. date: 1/26/09

Acknowledgements

I want to thank my son, Tom, for the help he has given me in preparing this manuscript; first by placing my longhand notes into his computer, then by editing the manuscript to shorten and improve the narrative and, finally, by searching through hundreds of photographs and selecting those that might enrich my narrative. He has graciously allowed me to add as an appendix his research into the genealogy of the Hafkenschiel family. I am most grateful.

Table of Contents

Part I
Memoirs

1.   The Early Years: 1916 to 1933

My mother was Anna M. Conroy, a native-born Ohioan. I was named after my father, Joseph Henry Hafkenschiel, also of Youngstown, who had been born in 1882 in the village of Cold Spring in Putnam County, N.Y. The original Hafkenschiels had emigrated from Holland. (There was a town in western Germany near the Netherlands border spelled HAFKENSCHEID which is the original source of the name "Hafkenschiel."). In the 1880 US Census there are listings for a C.H. Hafkenschiel who was a gunsmith, born in Holland, and his wife, Catharine, who was born in 1822 in Holland. Their son, Henry, my paternal grandfather, was born in South Carolina in 1852, probably shortly after the family had arrived in the US. His occupation was listed as "barber." My father had a younger brother who was killed in a railroad accident. I gather he was on the tracks of New York Central Main Line trains when he should not have been. He is buried in the family plot in Cold Spring. Thus, my cousins were all Conroy descendants.

My father had been working in New York in steel furniture

Joseph and Anna Hafkenschiel

production at the General Fire-proofing Company. He left Cold Spring, NY, having an eighth grade education, and was employed in Jamestown, NY by a steel furniture company. In the late 1890's, a group of Youngstown steel producers decided to have their own steel furniture manufacturing plant. They were able to entice some of the Jamestown principals to be the founding nucleus, and my father was asked to join them. Shortly after his arrival in Youngstown, he met his future wife, Anna, at a band concert They became engaged, and on Labor Day 1914, after a long courtship, were

3

married in St. Columba's Church. As part of their pre-marital agreement, they had resolved to save, purchase a lot, build, and furnish their own house before they married. They took up residence in their new house at 454 Lexington, which was not yet completely furnished.

Nate Conroy

I was born on April 2, 1916. My younger brother, Robert, joined the family on January 27, 1918. He was named after my uncle, Robert Flowers. In the Conroy family, there were nine daughters and two sons, several of whom died in childhood. The older son of Mark Conroy and Mary Joyce was named Mark Ignatius and was called "Nate." Nate was also employed at the Republic Steel Company, where his father worked as part of the security (police) force. Nate was invited by my parents to live with them at 454. This he did until he volunteered for active duty when the US declared war on Germany in 1917. He was shot in the spine in the battle of St. Mihiel, France, and died on Nov. 11, 1918. My mother never forgot this loss of her favorite brother.

The younger brother of Nate was Frank, who died soon after my mother in the mid '70's. His wife was Nan Holland and they had only one son, Richard. Richard was working in Youngstown and Cleveland for Ed DeBartolo (own SF 49ers), was married, and had two daughters.

Mark Conroy

I knew several of my mother's sisters. First, there was Geraldine who married a man named Carr. They had several girls and at least two sons named Mark and Joe. Mark joined Frank Conroy's plumbing team and, when Frank went to Italy (1929-1934), he ran Frank's plumbing business on the south side of Youngstown. The next older sister was Margaret who married Bob Flowers. They had no children. Nora was older than Margaret and she married Ed Butler. He was in the steel business and worked in Warren and Cleveland, Ohio, New York City, Washington DC and Japan. He served as a steel executive consultant on General Macarthur's post war occupation (1945) of Japan. Their children were Mary Louise, Ed, Bill, Jim, and Jeanne (now Deramee.) The only living relative now is Jeanne Butler

With Uncle Frank

Deramee of Thibodaux, Louisiana. Ed is a graduate of Annapolis (same class as Jimmy Carter) and is a lawyer and a banker. I don't know about their family, but on a visit to San Francisco, Lucinda and I had dinner with them, while Jimmy Carter was president. We exchange Christmas cards. The next younger sister was Frances. She was married to George Berger and they had two sons, George and Jack. Jack went to California and might have worked in Hollywood.

Soon after the war, my parents were able to buy a used car. My mother drove our father to work and picked him up each evening. He turned his paycheck over to my mother to manage the budget and save. In September 1921 (after my mother's visit to the school principal), I was allowed to enter the first grade class (there were two sections) in the Parmalee School. This was part of the public school system of the Youngstown City Board of Education. The school

Bob and Me on a Pony

system in Youngstown was started soon after the Civil War with the Rayen School in center city. Later the newest high school, built in the 1920's on the north side (where Lexington and Parmalee schools were situated), was named Rayen High School. The old Rayen School building was converted for use as the Board of Education offices. The Parmalee School was located a furlong walk from 454 Lexington, at the corner of Belmont and Broadway. I was put in class 2A, skipping the beginning of the second year, having had my 6th birthday the previous April.

All was going well with the family until 1923 when Bob, at age 5, became ill on a Friday evening and died 48 hours later. This was due to ischemia of the small bowel from an adhesion which occluded the arterial blood supply to the intestine. This led to necrosis and exsanguination. If the surgeons had operated and transfused, he might have survived longer than his 5+ years. This tragedy was heartbreaking for the family. My only reminders

Posing With My Brother Bob

of Bob are several pictures of him taken by an itinerant photographer early in his fifth year. These are now owned by Wendy and Tom because, of my four sons, Tom, as a five year old, reminded me most of Bob. My parents were sensitive to the fact that this was not only their loss, but also mine. The summer of 1923 they sent me to a nearby camp, Camp Stafford in Ravenna, Ohio. This was operated by my father's Knights of Columbus group and was enjoyed by an older cousin, George Berger, whose mother was the next younger sister of my mother. Her name was Francis Conroy. I was very unhappy there. My cousin understood this and arranged for his parents and mine to come and take me home after the first week.

That September, my parents, practicing Roman Catholics, decided that I should go to the parish school for my fourth grade studies. I was enrolled in St. Columba's primary school, which was located near the church, in downtown Youngstown. This required a ten minute bus ride from the corner of Lexington and Ford

Avenues southward to center city. In the class of 4th graders, I became acquainted with Regis Gilboy and John Stotler who became lifelong friends. I lost touch with them after my mother's death in 1965, the occasion of my last visit to Youngstown. I did well in class work, played touch football and basketball, and occasionally walked the 3 miles home from school after basketball practice with the Columban Meteors, a team in class D of the Youngstown City Playground League.

Although her father had steady work in the security group of Republic Steel Company, my mother had taken a job in the Mahoning County Court House. Her assignment was keeping record of real estate transactions for the county tax collector and the recorder of deeds. After her marriage at age 22 she gave up her job, but maintained contact with the bankers and real estate agents she met in the seven years that she worked at the courthouse. Through one of these contacts, she learned of a house for sale which had been repossessed by a local bank. It was located further north in Youngstown, at 225 Curry Place, an area with good schools. Her banker friend knew of her good credit standing and arranged for them to buy this nearly new house for a small down payment and regular affordable payments thereafter. Because the house was empty, she was anxious to move, and, having found a renter for 454 Lexington that she believed reliable, convinced my father to move to 225 Curry Place.

My mother's parents had lived at 125 Wellendorf (later Benita) Avenue near Curry Place, the St. Edwards Church, and the new Rayen High School (which was the premier school for students whose

225 Curry Place

parents were planning to enroll in college). Mary Joyce Conroy, my maternal grandmother, was dysfunctional because of alcoholism, and had been cared for in an out-of-town sanatorium. After her death, my grandfather, still working, decided to accept my mother's invitation to join our family at 225 Curry Place but insisted on paying rent and continuing work.

Because the St. Edwards' parish school had a good reputation, and was also across the street from the new Rayen High School, my mother arranged for me to join the fifth grade class there in September 1924. My teacher in the 5th grade at St. Edwards was Sister Kevin. She was very strict and insisted on mastery of the basics. I did well, competing with outstanding scholars such as Lillian Billock and John M. Newman.

Having completed the eighth grade, I graduated in June 1929 and planned to enter Rayen High School, not more than a ten minute walk from 225 Curry Place. The most important part of the last two years at St. Edwards was my membership in the parish Boy Scout troop #28 with Scoutmaster Mike Flanagan, assistant Paul Gilronan, and troop committee man, Mike Sweeney. This is how I later met Dan Gribbon who went to Rayen in 1930 and Joseph Lutz Flynn who entered Rayen in 1931.

As I entered Rayen, I had the choice of an academic course or a technical course (machine shop, printing shop, typewriting, etc.). Because of the contacts with our family physician, Dr. Morrison, a graduate of University of Pennsylvania Medical School, and my mother's "original plan" of becoming an R.N., as well as my curiosity regarding the death of my younger brother, I was already considering "pre med" and so I took the academic subjects that were suggested. These included: Latin (Miss Smith), German (Miss Richards), English (Miss Maguire), History (Mr. Tear) and Sciences (which were an introduction to chemistry and physics) and mathematics (Miss Doerschuk). Miss Maguire gave me a B in 1930. Outstanding scholars were Dorothy Brackett, Lillian Billock, Frances Rosenblum, John Newman, John Stotler and Regis Gilboy. I was on the Honor Roll at graduation in June 1933, having all A's except that B in English my first year. However, my rank in class was #3, Lillian Billock and Dorothy Brackett having received all A's.

My father and mother always lived on the north side of Youngstown. They were still living at 225 Curry Place when I went to Swarthmore in Sept. 1933. Early in 1934, the tenants of 454 Lexington moved out. My mother convinced my father and grandfather that they should move back to 454 Lexington and either rent or sell 225 Curry Place. Fortunately, a buyer was found before they moved and a profit was made on the sale. I remember being at Lexington with my grandfather who was now blind, following a stroke. My high school friends would come and meet me. My grandfather Conroy enjoyed being introduced to Dan Gribbon, Hank Cantwell, Jimmy Patrick, John Stotler and Regis Gilboy. He would quiz them about their parents and grandparents, many of whom he knew. We continued to live there after his death in 1938. Soon after his funeral, one of my older cousins, Edward T. Butler, Jr., whose mother and father were living in Cleveland Heights, Ohio, was transferred from his Cleveland Erie Railroad job to Youngstown. My mother invited him to stay with us as long as he wanted. He soon brought a colleague, and they lived there for several years, continuing even when I was at Johns Hopkins Medical School.

In 1939, a real estate friend of my mother's told her about a house at 360 Fairgreen near the corner of Ford Avenue. My mother bought that house and was able to sell 454 Lexington at quite a profit, moving in while I worked the summer of 1939 in Pathology at Hopkins. In that same year, her attention was called to a duplex on Elm Street further out on the north side than the Curry Place location. With the proceeds of the Lexington sale she was able to make the (sizable) down payment and allow the tenants to stay at their same rental rate. This property remained in the family and was only sold after my father's death in 1971. My parents remained in the Fairgreen Avenue house during the war years from 1941-1945. Sometime in 1948, after my father retired, my mother was able to buy a house at 1337 Fifth Avenue, selling the house on Fairgreen. She and my father lived there until her death in 1965. Lucinda and I visited them there at least once with all four sons. That house was sold sometime in 1966 when I had joined Sandoz.

While we were living at 454, my mother was friendly with Tom Pemberton, who ran a sporting goods shop in downtown Youngstown. He suggested that my family should get me a membership in the YMCA. This modern building was almost next door to his store. I went there on Saturdays and was in a basketball and swimming class. One outside activity was an outdoor "run." I entered that and won the "under 10" race. Soon after moving to 225 Curry Place and entering St. Edwards School, I found that boys in my grade were playing tennis and softball there. It was about a mile walk, but I went there after school and on weekends. Eventually, I had my own racquet and balls and found that I was asked to play more.

In the spring of 1926, my father took a job with a friend -Tom McLaughlin-at Truscon Steel. The work was more varied than the production of steel furniture and shelving at General Fireproofing as this company had a large market share of steel railings that were used along the side of highways. Soon after joining, my father was invited by Tom McLaughlin and Paul Arons, two of his superiors, to join the Truscon team in the golf league that they were starting.

As the weather changed, a group of contemporaries from Crandall Park would go to the "Y" and be in a league of under 16 years and play other teams. Eventually, the Crandall Juniors team members were recruited to play in a "playground class D league" that Tom Pemberton as City Recreation Director had organized. After leaving St. Edwards, I was not big or skillful enough to play high school basketball. Instead I played with the Columban Meteors in the class D organized basketball league . This is where I came under the influence of Nick Johnson, son of a janitor, who played tennis and basketball at Rayen High School. He devoted his free time to sports for young people; while unmarried, he earned a living by washing windows in downtown stores. Nick was hired by St. Columba's parents to manage the basketball court which was in the old church in downtown Youngstown. Nick recruited me, as well as Dan Gribbon, to play with his Columban Meteors who had a history of winning the class D title. I played with this team until I turned 17 in the spring of my last year at Rayen and was captain that final year. Unfortunately we never won a city championship.

It was common for St. Edwards students to use Crandall Park for after school activities. While in the 7th and 8th grades, football pick-up games were played on the school grounds and at Crandall Park. As 8th graders there were enough to have two teams that would play against each other and occasionally schedule a game with boys who lived not as far north as Crandall Park. It was when I was a freshman at Rayen, and too small for high school football, that the father of one of our players took an interest in our play and volunteered to help get us organized. The motivation for this was the publicity that a team of the same age and weight had received from the nearby town of Kent, called the "Kent Bearcats." They had played a team in Charlottesville, Virginia called "The Fives" and beat them. Someone of our group had written to Kent, the team being backed by Martin L. Davey, a "tree surgeon," whose son was on the team. The Kent Bearcats' manager wrote back and suggested that a game might be arranged at some time in the future, if an appropriate site in Youngstown could be obtained. Edward T. Mac Donall, father of our teammate, and former coach of Louisiana State University, took up the challenge and made the arrangements.

We played the Kent Bearcats the next football season in the Stadium of Youngstown South High School and were badly beaten, but received some favorable publicity in relation to younger aged football players. The following season, Nick Johnson told me that a team was being formed by Paul Green, a local business man, and this team was to be coached by Dyke Beede, an alumnus of Carnegie Tech, now Carnegie Mellon, who had coached at a small college, Geneva, before returning to Youngstown to sell insurance. Nick was his assistant. I made the squad and played as quarterback in neat uniforms in Kent, Ravenna and Youngstown.

When I was in the seventh grade, but not yet 12, my mother told me that her friend, Mike Flanagan, a member of St. Edward's church and scoutmaster of Troop 28, had told her that he would like me to attend meetings and see if I was interested enough to enroll after my 12th birthday. This is how I started going to the troop meetings, one night a week. I liked the leaders, Mike Sweeney and Paul Gilronan, and was able to pass all the tests for tenderfoot rank before my 12th birthday arrived. I completed the tests after 2 April 1928 and was awarded my first (tenderfoot) badge. My interest continued and my mother arranged for me to go to scout camp which I did, in the summers of 1928, 29, 30, 31, 32 and 33, eventually becoming a counselor. My participation advanced me to senior patrol leader and Eagle rank with 36 merit badges. Dan Gribbon and Joe Flynn were fellow scouts.

In April 1933, I did not know where I would go to college. I was aware that Regis Gilboy was going to go to Ohio State, John Newman to University of Pittsburgh, and John Stotler to John Carroll in Cleveland. I had invited Rosemary Gribbon as my date for the Rayen Senior Prom. Her brother Dan, my friend from Boy Scouts, and teammate in basketball and football, was in his third year at Rayen. He had taken several classes with Mr. Tear in which he had done well. Mr. Tear asked Dan if he would like to go to High School Senior Weekend at Oberlin, his alma mater. Dan asked me to go with him and inquired if I would be able to get my parents' car inasmuch as I, at 17, was of driving age. My mother and father gave their permission and Dan asked Mr. Tear if he would introduce me as well. Mr. Tear agreed to this, and arranged for us to be housed in a fraternity as Oberlin guests. Dan and I drove the 60 miles to Oberlin on a Friday afternoon and found the fraternity house. There we met our host, the captain of the basketball team, and he showed us our room and the dining room and told us where the HQ was and how to get there. That was the last we saw of him. Dan and I were left to explore the campus on our own and returned home on Sunday.

I reported favorably to my mother and father and we went over the papers needed to apply for admission and scholarship aid. My mother helped me complete the application and we mailed them to Oberlin. My mother remembered an active Brown alumnus who had played football at Brown. She called him and he asked her to send me to his office. I went there the next Saturday and told him I wanted to take a pre-med course. I told him what I had done in Scouting and Athletics and what I thought was my class standing. He gave me applications to complete, including scholarship aid. These were put in the mail, but only after another surprise interview intervened.

The Wednesday after Dan and I returned from Oberlin, Miss Richards, my German teacher for 3 years, asked me to come see her after classes. Using the Quaker "plain" language, she said,

"I understand from Mr. Tear that thee has been to Oberlin. I want thee to know about my college, Swarthmore." She said she would recommend me to compete for the "open scholarship" at Swarthmore. An interview at Swarthmore was necessary. Would I be interested and would my parents agree? I said I would report back the next day. My parents agreed and Miss Richards did all the paperwork and gave me the date and time of the interviews before the admissions and scholarship committees.

I took the overnight Greyhound bus to Swarthmore and in Philadelphia went to the "Y" as Miss Richards suggested, cleaned up and took the train out to Swarthmore. I was assigned a guide to show me around and I had the interview in the President's house. The guide was a member of the Phi Delta Theta fraternity and he (Robert Lewis-class of '35-captain of lacrosse) showed me a wonderful time. He took me to a member's house in Swarthmore Village after dinner and the member's sister, a high school senior, had some friends there who entertained me. We talked and listened to records. "Stormy Weather" was the big hit. I was impressed with the beauty and concentrated aspects of the Swarthmore campus and the cordiality of everybody I met. This was as different from Oberlin as day is from night. My trip back home was uneventful and I told my mother and father that Swarthmore was where I would like to go. Necessary papers were completed. I was fortunate to learn in the next few weeks that I had offers of scholarships to Brown and Oberlin and a letter from Swarthmore that I did not get "the open" but I did get a tuition scholarship and a chance to earn room and board by working in the dining room.

I was thrilled with the prospect of college work at Swarthmore. The village was small and most attractive. The college was set apart on a hill to the north, but well within the northern boundary of the village. It had been the academic starting place of a favorite Rayen teacher, Edna Harriet Richards. Her family were Quakers and she had graduated in 1898, obtained her PhD in Berlin, and returned to Swarthmore as a teacher and Dean of Women from 1918 to 1921. It was my good luck that she returned home after her mother died and served as a housekeeper for her two brothers who were bachelor farmers. She told me that she had soon become bored and had obtained the teaching position in German at Rayen. I accepted the Swarthmore offer in late May and plans were set to go there in early September. That summer was my last as a Boy Scout camper, joining a Rover Scout program conducted by Herman Brandmiller, Harvard '33.

2. Swarthmore College: 1933-37

Soon after 1933 Labor Day, my mother drove me to the Greyhound station in Youngstown. I boarded the bus that was going to Philadelphia by way of Pittsburgh via Route 30 to Philadelphia. I had all my possessions in one large suitcase. My mother had purchased a plastic suitcase in which she mailed extra underwear, pajamas and shirts. The four hundred mile trip took 12 hours as there was a stop every two to three hours. When we arrived in Philadelphia, I got on the local train to Swarthmore.

Having traveled all night, it was early morning when I alighted with my heavy suitcase at the Swarthmore station. I met another student, Sam Kalkstein on the station platform. He was also a freshman and was a graduate of Erasmus Hall high school in Brooklyn, New York. He told me he was on a scholarship and that he was going to major in Chemistry. We climbed the steps of the "Asphaltum" to Parrish Hall together. We saw much of each other, sharing Chemistry courses and Honors seminars. He was on the Varsity basketball team and was captain of lacrosse. He married a Swarthmore woman, Class of '39 and their sons were at Swarthmore with my sons. After registering at Parrish Hall, I learned that I was assigned to live, not in the all class men's dormitory, Wharton Hall, but in an off-campus house known as Woolman House. There were a total of 12 men living there, and our proctors were Professor and Mrs. Carl Spaeth, then at Temple Law School. His wife was a Scottish woman, Sheila Grant, and they had an infant son, Carl Grant Spaeth, whom they called "Puffy", pronounced as if "Poofy." He was perhaps 1 ½ years old, just beginning to walk, and still in diapers. His mother was rather casual and we all learned when, where and how to change diapers. This was a family that I was to see again as "Puffy" later went to Exeter and Stanford. He attended law school and practiced in Palo Alto. We were fellow members of San Francisco Golf Club. When he was president of the United States Golf Association and present at the 1989 U.S. Amateur Championship at Merion Golf Club, I had the pleasure of driving him out to Swarthmore and showing him around Swarthmore College campus faculty houses along with revisiting Woolman House. During the war years his father lived in a faculty house while he served in Washington with Nelson Rockefeller, a classmate of Carl's at Dartmouth. There Spaeth won a Rhodes scholarship and later earned a law degree at Oxford. Mrs. Spaeth was the niece of the Dean of Men, Harold Speight, at Swarthmore, and this was their connection and my good luck to meet them there.

At registration, I learned that there was no specific "pre-med" curriculum. This was up to the individual and his advisors. I was advised to major in Physiology-Zoology and to minor in Chemistry. For reasons I don't remember, I ended up taking Biology, Chemistry, The Romantic Movement (English), Math and German. Graduation requirements were four years of Latin which I was able to satisfy by passing an examination. My language was German and I was required to have three years of that. The test I took qualified me to satisfy the requirement by taking 1 ½ more years of College German.

My scholarship covered my tuition ($400) and housing in Woolman House ($200). For my board (3 meals a day), I was to assist in the kitchen and dining room on a one meal schedule which varied. This was equivalent to $300. I was taught how to wait on tables and that was mostly what I did. However, as part of my room, I had to assist in firing a coal furnace in the basement of Woolman House. My partner in this assignment was James E. Buckingham of York, PA. His room was on the first floor where the Spaeths lived. My single room was on the third floor.

The athletic facilities at the college were impressive, and a new "field house" on the lower campus was under construction. This was designed by an outstanding Philadelphia architect, Waller Karcher. Later, I was able to buy his home in Merion in 1952, a house he designed around an ADAM mantle. We were required to swim the length of one of the two pools (50 feet) before graduation. Every student was urged to participate in sports and I reported to the Men's Gym for the first football practice. There might have been some freshmen recruited for their athletic skills, but most of the squad were "walk-ons." I was given a uniform and became a member of the freshman team. The head coach was George Pfann-

Cornell '24-an All-American halfback and a Rhodes Scholar. Other coaches were alums: Vincent Schneider, Henry Parrish and Avery Blake who also coached lacrosse. The freshman team (Buckingham, Cooper, Peters, Spruance, Perkins, Worth, Clement and Anfinsen, had a two or three game schedule. The only game I remember was with the Episcopal Academy, then in Merion. We were bussed over to Philadelphia's City Line and played in a field in front of the school buildings. We were trounced 42-0 in a game in which most of the touchdowns were scored by a fleet halfback named Eddie Collins, Jr., son of the famous Athletics baseball player. In later life, I met a friend of Carol's, Frank Wetherill, who remembered playing on the line for Episcopal that day. He said when our second team came on the field, their team shouted, "Here come the intellectuals!"

My five courses were challenging and almost defeating. It was

Football at Swarthmore

evident that my classmates were better prepared than I, even with the good teaching I had at Rayen. Their reading knowledge was greater, they wrote better, and many had already taken courses in calculus. Not only was I struggling with my class and laboratory work, but I was also having what I now look back on as "allergic rhinitis." I seemed to be susceptible to head colds and came under the care of the college physician, Dr. Gillespie. He examined me in his office at the Men's Gym and, because of my nasal congestion, he suggested that he could treat me better in his Swarthmore Village office. There he put swabs of cocaine in my nostrils which seemed to shrink the swollen turbinates. I slept soundly after those treatments.

During the first Christmas vacation that year my mother took me to an ENT specialist in Youngstown. He subjected me to a surgical procedure, removing a turbinate and an adenoid, but I was little improved.

My first semester grades were not good, but I felt well enough in the spring to go out for baseball and played on the freshman team as a right fielder in the few games that the team had before "spring break." At the time of the spring vacation in 1934, I was able to arrange with the Swarthmore grounds foreman to get a WPA job rolling the clay tennis courts and other odd jobs. Because the dining hall was closed, I was able to arrange a dishwashing job at the village restaurant so that I would get an evening meal. The food there was better than at the College and I made many friends by the association there with the Kurtsall family of Ingleneuk fame.

The outdoor work and rest from class work during that vacation, as well as some urging by a classmate, Manning Amison Smith, resulted in my decision to give up baseball and, instead, jog with Manning after our Chemistry labs, 4-5 days weekly. I reported to the track coach, Bert Barron, and he provided me with a uniform. I ran the mile in several meets. My times improved over the last six weeks of the second semester and I did better in my tests. However my grades the second semester were not adequate to allow me to remain in the category of a "scholarship student." I knew when I left for Youngstown that I was going to lose my support because of my mediocre academic work.

Prior to returning to Youngstown, there was an opportunity for me to work at the College helping to prepare for Alumni Day which followed the end of exams. I volunteered and believe my volunteering to work during spring vacation and preparing for Alumni Day accrued to my advantage although my grades did not.

After I arrived home, my father had arranged for me to be interviewed for employment where he worked at Truscon Steel Company in the eastern part of Youngstown. I was given a job for the summer using a calculator to tabulate shipping weights. It was not very exciting work, but the pay was good and my mother drove my father and me back and forth. The people were all helpful and I felt appreciated at the company, and was encouraged by my very first job in the industrial world. Not more than a week after I started at Truscon, my mother handed me a letter from the Swarthmore

Dean. My scholarship had been cut in half, that is, $200 towards the $400 for the year. The challenge was whether my family could make up the $200. Nothing was said about financial aid for room and board. Nor was there any mention made of working on the grounds for a WPA subsidy/a federal grant program, which I had done during the previous spring vacation.

We were living at 225 Curry Place on the north side of Youngstown. Mark Conroy, my mother's father was living with us. I was trying to get caddy jobs on the weekend, but there was too much competition for the few jobs. My mother and father were uncertain about what was possible. Fortunately the Lexington House was rented, satisfactorily, so it seemed.

A joint decision was made to delay a reply to the Swarthmore offer in order to explore the costs of entering the sophomore class of the liberal arts college of Ohio State University. Several of my Rayen classmates had enrolled there, and one of my best friends, Regis Gilboy, had enjoyed a good freshman year there. Regis helped me to apply and, very soon, after submitting my Swarthmore report card, I was accepted. The costs were such that my mother, still the business person of the family, decided they could be met. A deposit was made for my dormitory room and matriculation fee, and so, by early August 1934, I was looking forward to continuing my pre-medical training in Columbus, Ohio. My Truscon pay checks were turned over immediately to my mother as well as allowances that my grandfather gave me (he had retired by this time). My social life was minimal, but I did play golf with my father, uncle, and my peers.

Soon after the alternative to Swarthmore was finalized, I wrote to my classmates, Manning Smith and Jim Buckingham, to tell them that I would be transferring to Ohio State. Buckingham and I had done a good job with the furnace, the winter of 1933-1934 having been one of the coldest in history, and whether he, also a scholarship student, shared that with someone in the administration, I do not know.

I worked at Truscon up until the Labor Day weekend and was prepared to go to Columbus with Regis Gilboy later in the month. A few days after Labor Day, my mother received a call from the business office at Swarthmore inquiring about my status. She told the calling party that she was uncertain about our ability to pay $750 and more for a second year at Swarthmore. Since the yearly cost at Ohio State was much less, that was where I had arranged to go. That ended the phone call.

Soon afterwards, we received a letter from the Swarthmore business manager, Nicholas Pittinger. His letter stated that Swarthmore had reconsidered the half tuition offer and was now offering a full tuition ($400) scholarship. Also, the business office had arranged with the dining room that I would work there as a waiter for two meals a day, having worked only one the previous year, and that I would get full board covered ($300). He also wrote that a widow in Swarthmore, at 213 Elm Avenue, wanted a student to live with her and her aged father. I might have to do some lawn work and help with the furnace chores for my room for the year. That saved us $200. I was instructed to "Please notify if acceptable."

I changed all my Ohio State plans and, within a few days, I was on my way to Swarthmore so I would arrive on the same day that my classmates were required to report. This surprise action by the administrator, Nick Pittinger, whom I barely knew suggests to me that somebody in the supervisory category of maintenance must have put in a good word for me in addition to the good-spirited Dean Everett Hunt. Nicholas Pittinger was a wonderful man. I later learned that he did similar good deeds for many other students and faculty. Getting a second chance to succeed at Swarthmore was a maturing experience for me. I believe that I changed from a shy, inward-looking individual to one better able to be in touch with, and to help others: a quality that the Boy Scout years had taught me, but that I had seldom implemented.

In my second year at Swarthmore, the faculty changed the curriculum to a four course plan. I took Physiology, Physics and Math. After completing my German requirement, I took a semester of Economics. I was at Swarthmore in time for the first football team practice. I decided that I would go to the Men's Gym and see if I would be given a uniform. This was because I had great admiration for our coaches the previous year: all of whom had returned: Blake,

Parrish and Schneider. George Pfann had been recruited by Frank Aydelotte, the College President, to come to Swarthmore from his job as a prosecuting attorney in New York City for the fall season. Aydelotte was a Rhodes Scholar from Indiana University and was the chief executive at that time of the Rhodes Scholar Program in America. I believe that this "all-around man", a scholar, athlete, and gentleman, was the ideal at Swarthmore from his arrival in 1921 until he left to go to the Advanced Study Institute in Princeton in 1938.

There were not many Rhodes Scholar, all-American, prosecuting attorney football coaches in the United States during the Pfann years. Pfann and the college physician, Dr. Gillespie, were friends, and in my freshman year, I had more contact with Pfann in Gillespie's office after dinner than I did on the practice field. I did get a uniform and played in the backfield as a 'ball handler' and blocking back in the single wing offense. There were two varsity teams and two "scrub" teams and we practiced as the opposition for the coming weeks "trick" plays as learned by Schneider's scouting. When an individual made a savage tackle or a brilliant run, he might be moved up to a better team, often temporarily. I recall that the best showing of the varsity that year was the defeat of Amherst 7-6 at Swarthmore. The first time I played in a game was the next year at Amherst. They were beating us 40-6, when the coaches put everyone on the bench into the game. Flynn, then at Amherst, later gave me his program for the game on which I was identified as the starting quarterback for Swarthmore.

My academic work was better, and I had more confidence in my ability to do the work necessary to master the subject matter. Our family finances were also better and, although I was living a 10-15 minute walk away, my family agreed to finance my joining the Kappa Sigma fraternity. Jim Buckingham and Manning Smith were members and this allowed me to have more interaction with Swarthmore women socially than I had in classes my freshman year. At that time I was a "rushee" and I recall that one of the senior Kappa Sigs, Reid McNeil, a 'smooth' dancer, was with me in the Parrish Hall after dinner informal dancing scene and told me he wanted to introduce me to Lucinda Buchanan Thomas, the best woman dancer in the college. We danced a few steps, not much was said, and another student cut in. By sophomore year, both Lucinda and Reid had graduated and I was always curious about which women could follow my steps, and who the best dancers were.

After the football season, I played on the Kappa Sigma basketball team in the inter-frat league season. Then I started jogging with Manning Smith to get in shape for the coming outdoor track season. The new field house was completed and there was a 1/8th mile cinder track that we used when the weather was stormy. The coach was Bert Barron again and he was planning to schedule indoor meets for the next season. By this time I was finding that I could do better in the half mile than the mile, though I attempted to do both at each meet. Manning Smith, a much better runner, encouraged me as we visited each other's homes the next summer, and we competed in Cleveland and in the AAU meets in Akron, Ohio.

Helmuth Kirschlager, '38, who had pledged to join Kappa Sigma was a big fellow, a fast halfback, was able to start many games his first year. He was a good 100, 220 and quarter mile track man and was living in Akron with his recently arrived German parents. He also competed in the summer meets locally for the next two seasons.

My grades in my second year steadily improved. Aydelotte had started the "Honors" program at Swarthmore. By the time I was a sophomore, and interested in graduate school, that was "the" course of study to pursue. This plan of study with small classes, two seminars each semester, and final exams after the third or fourth years to decide the "Honors" level, appealed to me.

At the end of the first semester of my second year I was bold enough to apply to read for "Honors" in my third year. To my surprise, I was accepted with '37 classmates, Earl Bendit, Ward Fowler, Richard Koenneman and Alba Helbing. All except Miss Helbing graduated from medical school. This study plan, with the smaller classes, allowed me to follow the examples of "Honors" upperclassmen. They had the privilege of using the Biology and Chemistry Department's libraries and, there, one could read current reports. Using the scientific journals and producing short essays on what I read helped me in my second year to do better in tests and term papers. At the end of my second year, my academic work was such that I was approved for "Honors", majoring in Physiology-Zoology and minor Chemistry.

In the second year, I worked on the grounds as well as in the dining hall. I also helped Mrs. Youmans with her garden and kept the house comfortably warm for her and her father. She indicated that she would like me to stay with her in the next academic year. Because the third year studying would be mostly in the Biology and Chemistry libraries on the campus, I accepted the opportunity to care for the animals that Dr. Walter Scott, the physiologist in the Biology Department, used for his experimental work and earned additional spending money to the one dollar that my mother sent me each week.

After I found that I had passed and was accepted academically for the third year, I volunteered to stay and help prepare for Alumni Weekend. At this time, I learned from Nick Pittinger that I had been approved for the same tuition and dining room support for my third year. He complimented me on being accepted for "Honors", and wished me good luck for the summer.

That summer, through Tommy Pemberton, the Youngstown City Playground Commissioner, I became the Playground Director at Victory Field on the east side of town. When I arrived home I found that my parents had moved back to 454 Lexington with my Grandfather Conroy. I renewed my friendship with high school classmates, played some golf and attended several softball picnics. When September came, I was in good health and physically fit as a result of my summer with the friends I made at Victory Field.

As I began the "Honors" program, I had more confidence in my ability to study on my own. Being in a seminar with four to six students, the Professor, and frequently a younger faculty member of his department, helped me to be better able to discuss what I had learned and to write more cogently. In the four seminars (two chemistry and two biology), we were examined at the end of the semester, but not given grades except to be admitted, or not, to Honors for my senior year. All in our pre-med group advanced. I was again able to help Mrs. Youmans and worked in the dining room, fed Dr. Scott's animals, worked on the grounds during spring vacation, and waited on tables at the Ingleneuk Tea Room in the village each evening during the spring vacation. Mrs. Youmans helped me to get a Pennsylvania driver's license and I was able to help her with shopping and occasionally drove her on longer excursions.

On one occasion I drove her to visit her son, Edward, at a Civilian Conservation Camp (CCC) near Williamsport in Central Pennsylvania. Edward was a graduate of Cornell, as was his 90 year old grandfather, whom I had helped care for at 213 Elm. The CCC was a federal program started by FDR in 1932 to care for State and Federal properties by giving young people jobs and educational opportunities; a chance to get "on-the-job" training in a structured setting much like military camp. Edward was selected as a Forester to help organize tree-planting projects. Mrs. Youmans asked me if I could free up a long weekend in the spring to drive her up to Williamsport to visit Edward and see the CCC. Edward had arranged to stay with us at a private home that was operated as a B&B for guests during the deer hunting season in the autumn. The farmer's wife served us venison sausage with our eggs every morning. That is how I learned to like spicy food and still do. This trip gave me an insight into how fortunate I was to have the opportunity of a Swarthmore education and to better appreciate what was being done by the federal government to help our fellow citizens who had limited opportunities.

As I look back on that year, I think playing the game at Amherst; making trips to play Hamilton College in New York and Hampden Sydney College in Virginia, and the visit to the CCC were the most broadening experiences of my third year. During spring vacation, I again worked on the grounds, waited on tables at the Ingleneuk, and, after taking and passing the Honors exams, stayed on to help prepare for Alumni Weekend.

I returned to Youngstown in mid June to work again for the city at the Victory Field playground. This time I worked with a young woman from the west side of town who helped to organize activities for the young girls. I was learning to deal with all sorts of old and young people who came to the playground. The challenge was to lead them in games, to keep physically fit, and on rainy days, to play checkers and chess.

Mr. Oliver Ellis, a former gym teacher of mine at Rayen, drove me back and forth. He was supervisor of a playground nearby and I learned from him how to lead young people by example and to ostracize troublemakers. The summer flew by, and that year invitations were sent to upper class football, soccer and cross country team members to come back to college for an athletic training table one week before the upper classes were to begin. The Social Committee had invited me to join them and they, too, were invited to come back early to help with Freshman Orientation days. I was selected by my fellow Kappa Sigs to be their representative on the inter-fraternity council, a group that was also allowed to come early to make plans for the "rushing" season, which was usually completed by mid October.

I remember well one of my Swarthmore Biology Department Professors, Robert Enders whose particular interest was Embryology. He had worked in Baltimore at the Carnegie Institute before coming to Swarthmore. This facility was located on a section of the basic science quadrangle of the School of Medicine at Johns Hopkins University adjacent to the Johns Hopkins Hospital. Enders had interacted with some of the Hopkins basic science faculty; anatomists, histologists, embryologists. Knowing that the two most brilliant of our pre-med group, Bendit and Fowler, had their hopes set on getting scholarships to Harvard Medical School, Enders encouraged me to think of Hopkins as my first choice.

When I was home on vacation, my mother and father had arranged a visit with the Admissions Office of the Western Reserve University of the School of Medicine, in Cleveland, 65 miles away. I met the Professor of Physiology, Carl Wiggers, and, upon learning I was more interested in clinical medicine, he arranged for me to speak to two Professors of Medicine, Wearn and Heymans. Although they were Harvard Medical School graduates, they talked enthusiastically about their post-graduate work at Penn Medical School in the Pharmacology Department with Richards and Schmidt. When another biology professor at Swarthmore, Brooke Worth, MD, a graduate of Penn, encouraged me to think about that medical school, I remembered my visit with Wearn and

Heymans in Cleveland and resolved to apply to Penn as well as to explore Hopkins' possibilities.

Sometime early in my fourth year, Enders said he would contact the Hopkins Dean's Office and set up an appointment for me to be interviewed. My mother and father knew about Johns Hopkins Hospital and urged me to go "for the best" and that they would finance a visit there. Dr. Enders' inquiry resulted in Hopkins suggesting a Saturday in September to meet with the representative of their Admissions Committee at the Medical School.

Although I had been at football practice for only two weeks, I saw that the freshman recruits were talented and the new coach would be playing them on his starting team. I knew I would not be missed on the Hopkins designated weekend. I affirmed the suggested date and time and went to Baltimore by train.

My interview was assigned to Mr. Burgan who was older than my Swarthmore professors and was the Treasurer of the Medical School. He was not an MD, but he gave me a tour of the basic science campus and a brief visit to the roof of the hospital pointing out different departments and buildings. Mr. Burgan was very knowledgeable and kind, and he answered my questions well. We discussed the details of what the costs were and he gave me some ideas about where to live and get meals, since the medical school had no dormitories, other than the medical fraternities with their individual houses.

He tipped me off about a specific boarding house at 1013 N. Broadway. This I visited later that day and met the proprietor and said if admitted, I wanted to be with her. Mr. Burgan told me there was no financial aid to students, and I respected his open and simple manner. I told him I would like to pursue the details of applying for admission and explained to him something of the Biology "Honors" plan of study. He said he would introduce me to the Dean, Alan Chesney, MD, before I left. Dean Chesney was very pleasant, but for a young man, I realized he was deaf, wearing hearing aids and probably lip reading. He also assured me that I would be sent details of the formal admissions process.

On the trains back to Swarthmore, I realized what a fortunate bit of good luck I had in seeing Hopkins and meeting two principal figures in the operation of the Medical School. I wanted to make this place my first choice, but worried that financing that dream might not be possible. Within a week or so after I returned to Swarthmore, Dr. Enders told me that he had received a packet from the Dean's Office with an admissions form. He helped me complete that and wrote a formal letter of recommendation in his role as Chairman of the Biology Department. The letter also said that formal admissions requirements were: 1. A Bachelor's Degree; 2. Reading knowledge of Latin, German and French. This was to be tested by a written examination, when admitted, and on arrival on the campus the next September.

Dr. Enders, knowing my Latin and German background, said that he thought my lack of French would not be a problem. He suggested I contact Mr. Torrey of the French Department and ask for his help. This I did. I pursued his plan and he worked with me over the next six months; so that he was able to write a note telling the Admissions Committee of what I had accomplished under his tutelage.

Soon after the forms and a registration fee of $25 was sent, I received a letter from Dean Chesney saying that he would reserve a place for me in the September 1937 entering class, assuming I would be awarded a Bachelor of Science Degree from Swarthmore in June. This good news for me was known to others of the Biology Faculty. Dr. Worth said that the consensus was that I should apply to Harvard and Penn also, in order to "cover all bases." This I did and later was turned down by Harvard, but accepted by Penn.

The early encouragement by Hopkins gave me a great boost in confidence. I studied more effectively, did my chores with animals more carefully and enjoyed the seminars and my classmates more. "Honors" became fun, not drudgery.

Over the summer, I learned that the father of Mrs. Youmans had died and that she was going to change her residence. I contacted the Kappa Sigma President, my classmate, Fred Wiest, and asked if there was a possibility that I might be one of the two brothers allowed to room in the Kappa Sigma Lodge. I cited my case for financial help, based on no financial assistance from the Medical School I planned to attend. Soon I learned that I was to share the bedroom space with another brother, George Carson. The understanding was that for this privilege, we were to be vigilant, industrious, housekeeper-caretakers.

George Carson was an Engineering major who needed to work at the Westinghouse Plant on the Delaware, a full shift, 5 PM to 1 AM, five nights a week, in order to pay his tuition. I never knew when or where he ate. We worked well together and enjoyed the support that our Kappa Sigma brothers gave us. The Kappa Sigma Lodge had to be "ship-shape in Bristol fashion" for the Friday evening "table parties." A coed would be invited to dinner and escorted to the lodge for dancing and non-alcoholic refreshments. A faculty or administration member, usually an attractive woman and a good dancer, would be the chaperone. Another committee dealt with the selection and playing of the records that provided music for dancing. My recollection is that popular records were played over and over, but only one was played to signal that the party was over. That record was the "Stardust" music composed by our Kappa Sigma brother of Indiana University, Hoagy Carmichael. I always returned my date to her dorm as soon as the party was over at 9-9:30 PM. This year I served on the same committees (social and inter-fraternity council) as I did in my junior year. What was a special surprise (there was no campaigning on my part), was my election by classmates as Senior Class President for the first semester.

First Semester Officers

SCHROEDER, ELLIS, HAFKENSCHIEL, LEWIS

Class Officers

Later in our senior year, our permanent class president was William C.H. Prentice, who was still presiding at our 70th reunion. Bill lived with us in Woolman House our first year. He was one of the two Rhodes Scholars in our class, a Psychology major. He later became Dean of Swarthmore and later the President of Wheaton, Mass. College before retiring.

Looking back on the second semester of that fourth year, it seems that it was the best semester of all my Swarthmore years. I was in excellent physical condition, working on improving my time for the half-mile, a distance I concentrated on in my final year. I do recall that in the Haverford meet at Haverford, the score was close. I know that Lew Bose won it for Swarthmore, a Haverford man was a close second to Lew, and I beat out a Haverford man for third to get one point, which was our margin of victory.

My girl friends were varied and there were no romantic ties: Barbara Brooks, Betty Dobson, Connie Smith and Kay White. My best friends were my pre-med classmates and Kappa Sigma brothers, Jim Buckingham and Manning Smith. Just before final exams, I remember Connie Smith and her mother arranged an elaborate dinner party at their Lansdowne home, and I think I was Connie's date.

All went well until the Honors exams, designed by outside examiners, to be followed by oral exams by those visiting faculty members. The weekend before the written Honors were to begin, I decided to join classmates in relaxing. On Saturday we gave the Kappa Sigma Lodge a thorough "end of the year" house cleaning. On Sunday, we had arranged to be driven to the Phillies baseball game, starting from the campus before lunch. We had all been to breakfast in the dining hall. I remember some food/drinks were consumed during the game by one or more of us. I had something to eat at a roadside food place on our return to campus. I did not eat the evening meal in the college dining hall.

During the night I remember getting down from the upper bunk to answer an urgent call, and I climbed back and slept soundly till daylight. After a light breakfast, I went to the Chemistry Department lecture hall to answer the questions posed by the outside examiners. I was answering the questions and after about an hour's work, I suddenly felt nauseated and became acutely ill with vomiting, diarrhea and feverishness. The proctor of the exam helped me get to the Men's Room. After being there for five minutes or more, I realized I would not be able to finish the exam. I asked to be allowed to go to the infirmary, which was arranged. The R.N. on duty recorded my temperature, pulse and blood pressure and put me to bed and alerted the college physician. After several bowel evacuations, I went to sleep. I awakened as the physician appeared on his afternoon rounds. Specimens of blood, urine and stool were examined and after the next day or two, it was noted that my skin and eyeball colors were yellowish. The diagnosis was catarrhal jaundice. Now it would be hepatitis, food poisoning.

Treatment was symptomatic and I was in bed most of the time and slept more than usual. After a week, I was allowed to have visitors. A Biology Department representative contacted me and inquired whether Professor Samuel Palmer, the Acting Department Head, (and who gave the Botany seminar in the last semester), might visit me. The physician and the nurse agreed, and Samuel Palmer came in the next day. We agreed that I was ready to be examined on my knowledge of Botany, Biology and Chemistry. We talked for more than one hour about what I had learned in the previous two years. Professor Palmer called me and said that the faculty had decided that I would graduate with a course degree. This result seemed to be logical as there was no way that I could get an "Honors" degree due to what must have been a viral infection that I acquired before the exams began. Having been admitted to Hopkins, this degree was all I needed.

By the time of graduation day in early June, I was able to receive my diploma with my classmates, and I have a snapshot of me standing with Jim Buckingham in our caps and gowns with diplomas in hand, to recall that happy day. My mother and father had been driven to Swarthmore by my Uncle George and Aunt Frances to join in the ceremony. My Uncle Frank and Aunt Nan's only son was born on that day. He was named Richard. I lost track of him as a resident in Youngstown when I went to California in 1965.

My family returned to Youngstown before I did. I am vague about how I informed Mrs. Ningard of 1013 N. Broadway, Baltimore, that I would be there in September to live in her boarding house, later fictionalized as "Miss Susie Slagle's." Also how I got back to Youngstown, where I planned to spend the summer.

My mother had explored the possibility of my working for the Water Department of the City of Youngstown. There was a crew of outdoor workers, and the supervisor had told her to have me meet with him when I returned. After a week at home, walking more each day, I was well enough to do manual labor and went to see "The Boss." He agreed to take me on, told me what to wear and where and when to report. That is how my career as a ditch digger began. The work gang were all helpful, and we did what was needed to supply water and repair sewers. I turned over my paychecks to my mother and was given a small allowance. I was able to renew friendships with Rayen High School classmates, Regis Gilboy, John Newman and Dan Gribbon, who were going to law school. Joseph Lutz Flynn was going to Amherst and then to Harvard Business School. John Stotler and Jimmy Patrick were going to medical school.

My maternal grandfather, Mark Conroy, was still living with us at 454 Lexington, and my mother had worked out a plan with him to pay for my Hopkins expenses so that I might earn an M.D. After working outdoors in July and August, I was more fit helping with heavy tools, and I was ready to go back to the academic world.

3.   Medical School: 1937-41

In early September, with a large suitcase and my used Bausch and Lomb microscope, I boarded the Baltimore and Ohio train for the overnight trip to Baltimore. A taxi took me to 1013 N. Broadway, and Mrs. Ningard told me that upper classmates of the Nu Sigma Nu medical fraternity had extended an invitation to me to meet them and their girlfriends after dinner that evening. That is how my life as a med student began, and I will expand on that in the next chapter.

Looking back, with the perspective of over 65 years, I realize that I was very fortunate to learn of Mrs. Ningard's boarding house. She was the only one who seemed to be operating one at the time I entered medical school. Having a single room of my own on the third floor, I could study alone with a minimum of interruption. Across the hall from me was Meyer Zeiler, whose father and uncle were physicians in Los Angeles. Meyer was in the Class of 1940, so we had a friendship of three years. When Meyer graduated, George Cartwright from Wisconsin took his room. Thus, I only knew George for a year.

Mrs. Ningard provided a good breakfast beginning at 0630 and dinner at 1800, with a second seating at 1845, if one was late. One year, before I came, a woman asked Mrs. Ningard if she could have dinner only, and at the second seating. Mrs. Ningard accepted her. However, she did not realize that while this woman waited in the parlor, she took notes about the conversations she heard. Later, her novel about Hopkins students and medical school was made into a movie, and Mrs. Ningard was known as "Miss Susie Slagle", the title of the book.

When I arrived in Baltimore in September of 1937, some members of the medical fraternity, Nu Sigma Nu, had heard from Mrs. Ningard of my expected arrival in the early afternoon. This group had their own boarding house across from the Hopkins Hospital in the 600 block on N. Broadway. Because they wanted to have a full house, they would "rush" new students in the attempt to have a financially stable year. Although they knew Mrs. Ningard's boarders might take only the noon meal, they tried to be in touch with all sixty men in our class of sixty-five to enhance their status as a National Medical Fraternity.

Soon after I arrived, I received a phone call from Alfred Hunt and Richard Roth. They welcomed me and asked me if I would join them after dinner for dancing and drinks at one of the hotels that featured dancing on Sunday evenings. I agreed. I had a fine time, and with three women, all nurses, and the two upper class Nu Sigs, the time passed quickly. I was, however, a bit of a "wet blanket," as I was the only one not having alcoholic beverages. This introduction to social life at medical school alerted me to the fact that alcohol and "fast women" were to play a more prominent role than what was the coeducational life at Swarthmore College.

During the "rushing" of the five national and one local of the six fraternities, I met the Nu Sigs many times and we were always cordial. However, I decided not to join any fraternity in the early formal four weeks of rushing. Only later did I join the Phi Chi to have a luncheon group and other social life. This was because of the friendship of two of my classmates who were boarders of Mrs. Ningard's, and who earlier had joined Phi Chi. They were William Higgins and Marshall Sanford, both Davidson College graduates.

After the exams in the Welch Library were completed to verify one's reading knowledge of Latin, French and German, classes began. All first year students took the same courses at the same time. The first trimester was Gross Anatomy, Embryology and Histology. The groups were divided into fours alphabetically. My partners at the dissecting table were Milton Gusack, Myron Helfrick, and Charles Herbert. Psychobiology lectures introduced us to Professor A. Meyer.

The "Honors" program at Swarthmore prepared me well for graduate school. I had learned to be curious and to study on my own. The Hopkins teachers were in and out of the Anatomy Lab and instructed us how to proceed, but only in general. Questions were asked and one had to pursue the information either from one's own textbook, such as Gray's Anatomy, or go to the library to study an Atlas or read a scientific journal. The instructor might ask the same question several days later, and there were always some in the group who knew the answer, and some who did not. No written exams were given, but it became clear to all of us which classmates were not only intelligent, but diligent students as well.

The second trimester was Biochemistry with an outstanding Department Chairman, W. Mansfield Clark, PhD. There were written exams and laboratory work by which we were graded. The third trimester was Physiology with another outstanding Department Chairman, Philip Bard. He was a Californian, a graduate of Thacher, Princeton, with his PhD from Harvard. This subject I liked best and this was to be the basis for my medical career.

In the Histology segment of the first year Anatomy course, one had to have his own microscope in order to study and identify the specimens presented by the instructors. Knowing this, I had arranged before I left Philadelphia to buy a second hand model from a scientific instrument store that serviced the Swarthmore Biology, Chemistry and Physics Departments.

During the first week or so of classes, there was much activity at the medical book store located across from the hospital, on Monument Street. Microscopes were also sold by the book store. I remember an upperclassman, Sam Asper, who was selling microscopes near there for another manufacturer. It was in this area that I met the representative of the Philadelphia Company, Williams, Brown and Earle. That was where I had bought my instrument. It was an awkward situation for him to sell on the sidewalk, and he asked me if I would represent them. I said yes, and started. Realizing that I should have the latest model, I was eager to volunteer. This was arranged, and I sold one or two that first year to my classmates. This man recommended that I continue, and the company provided me with the latest models, instructions and prices. This was so productive that I represented them all four years. I am vague about how I was able to get the list of entering students each year, which noted their home town and college background. Perhaps that was because the fraternities needed the list for "rushing." My salesmanship was based on my ability to know who was on the list when I met the incoming students in the bookstore area and to match those individuals with their background. That helped me make a few sales every year.

At the beginning of the third year, my frat upperclassmen made me the Phi Chi Rushing Chairman because I knew so many of the incoming first year men by name. At Mrs. Ningard's dinner table, I met several physicians who had completed their residencies and were at Hopkins for post graduate/fellowship studies. Two were internists, Ludwig Eichna and Robert Wilkins, and the third was a dermatologist, also on the medical school faculty at Penn. Ira Schamberg was a fellow in the Dermatology-Syphilology Department. Ludwig Eichna, whom I would consider my most important medical mentor, was living in Mrs. Ningard's best room; the one on the second floor facing the street. Ike was a graduate of Penn College and Medical School. He had completed his residency there as Chief Resident in Medicine. He wanted to know more about Vascular Physiology. He was in his second year of a fellowship with James Bordley, MD, in the Department of Medicine.

I had not been long at 1013 N. Broadway, when I learned that Ike, although a reserved man, who listened more than he talked, wanted to have a partner to play squash at the hospital's court located in the power plant building. I told Ike that I was not familiar with the game, there being no squash at Swarthmore and only handball courts at the Youngstown "Y." Ike said it was much like handball, which I had played, and he said he had an extra racquet and that he would introduce me to the game and show me how to get into the court, used usually only by MD's. This was the beginning of our friendship which went on for the three years that Ike was at 1013. He left to be a professor stationed at Bellevue Hospital in New York City as a member of the NYU Medical Facility.

Little do I remember about a local chapter of a national group called the Association of Medical Students. I only remember my classmates who were interested in this program. They were: Gruenberg, Jacques and Meyer. They also were interested in the Psychobiology Orientation of Professor Adolf Meyer. I joined them in auditing every elective he gave in the Psychiatry Department Curriculum.

All the medical fraternities had dances during the academic year and all fraternity members and their dates were welcomed by the host fraternity. There was a dance almost every other Saturday night. On other Saturday nights we went to the downtown theatre, The Ford, that staged plays. For 75 cents and a seat in the balcony, I saw Katherine Hepburn in "Philadelphia Story" and others such as Tallulah Bankhead in "The Little Foxes" and Alfred Lunt and Lynne Fontanne in "The Taming of the Shrew."

The problems I had with frequent upper respiratory infections were not as serious as they were at Swarthmore. But I did have enough trouble with them that I soon became acquainted with the Medical Student Health Facility. This was located in the outpatient department of the hospital. The physician was an internist-Dr. Nathan Hermann. He had a practice in Baltimore and his service was part time.

He referred me first to the ENT staff and there I met John Bordeley, MD, the younger brother of James Bordeley, MD, who was Chief of the Hospital's Hypertension Clinic. Dr. Bordeley examined and treated me and I recovered. He alerted me to a possible allergic background as the cause and I was evaluated by the Allergy Clinic's Chiefs Gay and Winkenwerder. At the end of the first year Dr. Bordeley operated on me and, at his suggestion, I arranged to spend the summer in Arizona. Three times weekly in my second year, I went to the Allergy Clinic to be desensitized. This I did for the next three years.

January 1938 was the final page in my maternal grandfather's life. Mark Conroy lived to age 91. I returned to Youngstown to attend his funeral mass. His youngest son, J. Frank Conroy, was the soloist. I still remember the "Ave Maria" he sang at that mass. His legacy to Anna M. Conroy Hafkenschiel for her care during the last twenty years of his life made it possible for my parents to finance my Hopkins and Hospital of Univ. of PA training, until 1 August 1942, when I went on duty as a 1st Lieutenant.

The desirability of a dry, warm, allergen-free environment to aid the recovery from a sinus drainage and repair of a deviated septum was first suggested by Dr. Bordeley and repeated by Dr. Winkenwerder. My friendship with Ed Jakle, Swarthmore '40, a native of Flagstaff, Arizona, led to the suggestion of contacting Leo Weaver, one of the first Arizona "dude ranchers." A response from Leo suggested that he would like to have me as a "handyman" on his Kaibib, north rim Grand Canyon, "dude" operation, if I would be willing to work for room and board and arrange for my own transportation to and from Arizona. I discussed this with my parents, and they agreed to finance me when they learned that my 1013 roommate, Meyer Zeiler, had offered to drive me to Arizona on his way home to Los Angeles after classes were over. This we did with another Angeleno, my classmate Frank Inui. We shared auto and meal expenses, and within five days, I was in Flagstaff.

Ed Jakle was part of a large family with no guest room space and he arranged for me to stay with Ed Babbitt, a widower and family friend. I stayed with Ed for several days until Leo Weaver arrived to drive me up across the Colorado Bridge to Big Saddle, a seasonal hunting camp on the north side of the Grand Canyon. There I helped Leo and his wife entertain the paying guests for several weeks. When the guests required more action, the entire operation was moved, including ten horses, to Lee's Ferry on the Colorado. After the first group of guests left, no more "dudes" signed up, and I spent the rest of the summer helping Leo and his wife with chores on their "home ranch."

Within a few weeks, I was aware that my upper nasal passages were more open. The Zeilers wrote and invited me to be their guest at their beach house on Manhattan Beach, California.

I arranged for Leo to drive me to Flagstaff where I boarded the "Super Chief" to Los Angeles. The Zeilers and my classmate and fellow Phi Chi member, Willard Goodwin '41, entertained me for ten days. This was a wonderful experience, including meeting Sinclair Lewis. Soon it was mid August. I took the "Super Chief" to Chicago, and the Baltimore and Ohio to Youngstown.

Mexico 1938

I spent ten days with my mother and father, then living at 360

Fairgreen. I could not wait to get the train back to Baltimore, feeling healthier than I had been for the last two years.

My first activities on arriving at 1013, were to get organized to sell microscopes to the incoming first year students, having worked out an arrangement with both the bookstore and the 4ᵗʰ year student, Sam Asper, that I would be the only seller of a newer, more expensive German-made microscope. The commission on this sale was greater, and I was lucky enough, during "rushing" for Phi Chi, to sell three of the superior scope models.

The first trimester was in the Pathology Department with Professor MacCallum and Arnold Rice Rich. We viewed post-mortem examinations of patients who died in the Hopkins; one was Chick Webb. Tissue obtained from these dissections was prepared for examination under the microscope. Groups of four students were instructed by two faculty members, one, the daughter of one of the most prominent merchant families in Baltimore and a Hopkins graduate, and the other a recently hired M.D. from Canada, Joseph MacManus. The highlight of the week was a mid-day Wednesday Clinical Pathological Conference (CPC) conducted by the internist, Louis Hamman, and the pathologist, A.R. Rich.

Dr. Rich was an authority on the Pathology of Tuberculosis (TB), having written the standard reference. Although Dr. Rich and Dr. MacCallum were at that time not directly involved with the students, I sought Dr. Rich's counsel on the problem of early diagnosis of TB in medical students. This was on the agenda of the National Student Organization, the Association of Medical Students. Out of this interest, I learned that there had never been such a program at Hopkins, and, without a thorough search of the literature, I was unable to find any studies of:

1.   What other medical school students were experiencing;
2.   What the evidence suggested as to the desirability of earlier and earlier detection and treatment?

At that time there was no National Organization of Student Health Physicians, but Dr. Rich suggested that an approach to finding out what was being done might be discovered by a questionnaire to the Dean's Office of All United States Schools of Medicine. I said I would try to organize such, and that I hoped he might critique my efforts. That is what I did, and it led to a report in the Journal of Medical Students Association before I graduated. The prospect interested me enough that I arranged to attend the annual meeting of the Association held that year in Detroit during Christmas vacation. I stayed with the family of Richard Heavenrich, Swarthmore '37. Contacts made there facilitated getting my efforts published in an issue of their Journal. While I was at Hopkins, I saw no change in the policy and procedures of student health to pick up early TB by Dr. Hermann. But before I graduated, I was aware that the School of Medicine appointed, on a full time basis, one of the brightest young interns, R. Charmichael Tilghman, who had a part time assignment in the Dean's Office. This was probably a coincidence, not cause and effect!

This project continued into the second and third trimester when we had:

1. Study Pharmacology
2. Our life history for Psychobiology reviewed individually for at least one hour by the professor, Dr. Adolf Meyer
3. Introduction to Clinical Medicine with physical diagnosis methods practiced on each other.

In the final trimester, the emphasis was on Pharmacology, physical diagnosis, and observing, in pairs, third year students as they interacted with expectant mothers in the hospital neighborhood who had signed up for pre and post-natal care and home delivery.

Pathology in that period was limited to weekly 90 minute conferences with Professor MacCallum. Each week he selected a topic (usually covered in the textbook), but which was a surprise to the students any given week. Early in the last trimester, during the weekly quiz session conducted by Professor MacCallum, he began to "sound out" my classmates on the several theories of the clinical and usually fatal "shock syndromes." Classmates were asked to comment. Several did, but MacCallum continued to pursue what other ideas were known. I volunteered that I knew of a recently advanced theory of Pathologist Virgil Moon of Hahneman Hospital which I summarized for the class. Dr. MacCallum seemed surprised that a student would know about and have read a monograph which had not yet been officially catalogued for the Welch Library for general use.

I knew about the book because a few weeks earlier my fellow lodger and mentor, Ludwig Eichna, MD, had told me that he was reviewing a new book given to him by the Welch Library. His Chief, James Bordley, MD, had asked him to read it and write a review for the journal, "Bulletin of the Johns Hopkins Hospital." Eichna had let me have the book. I finished reading the book in a few days, and then wrote an outline of what was the evidence for the theory. Because Eichna wanted another viewpoint, we had a discussion of what I thought about this idea of vascular reactivity, related to the fall in blood pressure and the death of the patient I had no idea that this exercise would come to the attention of my teachers.

I suspect that this chance reading and class discussion had something to do with my being selected as one of five of the class of '41 chosen for summer studies in the Department of Pathology. Also on the list as were Austrian, Chinard, Palmer and Stewart Later, I came to understand from upper classmates that this was an important student opportunity. I shared the good news with my parents who agreed with my wish to take advantage of the opportunity. Somehow financial backing was provided, and this summer experience of doing autopsies, working on the reports and preparing the slides was my small contribution to the Pathology Department's international reputation for detailed scholarship in the field.

Mrs. Ningard had several other students and postgraduate MDs staying with her that summer. Because of the humid heat, my evenings were often spent in the nearby movie theater which was air-conditioned. Each admission was accompanied by a gift dish which we turned over to Mrs. Ningard and were seen again with my meals there over the next two years. Soon it was late August and I stayed in Baltimore and prepared for the sale of new microscopes and my assigned duty by the Phi Chi brothers to organize our group for the four week rushing period of September '39.

The first semester consisted of clerkships on the medical (Osler) wards. Four students supervised by an assistant resident did the history on each new patient. Then the intern would do the same plus a complete physical examination, and write up a separate entry note on the chart, and set up the orders for treatment and subsequent studies. The student had to have his or her write-up approved or revised before the teaching assistant resident would allow it to be a part of the clinical chart in the permanent record for the hospital files.

The next morning on "the rounds" with the attending and junior attending, the student would present the patient's history, physical and lab work without notes. The Chairman of the Department, Warfield T. Longcope, would make separate rounds, and much the same order was required. While listening, Dr. Longcope would shift his weight from left leg to right leg. When he spoke, he seldom uttered anything special or forceful. His "nickname" was "shifting dullness."

Down the hierarchy of the Department of Medicine were such luminaries as Ben Baker, Maxwell Wintrobe, George Thorn and Chief Resident, A.M. Harvey, who became Chairman of the Department in the post World War II years. Outstanding teachers were W. Barry Wood and Palmer H. Futcher, both Hopkins '36 and Josh Billings, '37. One of the interns, Alfred Florman, was a former boarder at 1013. It was his patient that came to post-mortem examination the previous summer. Because our pathological workshop identified the causative organism, Rickettsia in Rocky Mountain Spotted Fever, we collaborated in a report in the Hopkins Bulletin.

The second trimester was on the Surgical (Halstead) Wards. The workup of the new patients was much the same as in the Department of Medicine. The famed chairman, Dean Lewis, who retired and died three years earlier, had not yet been replaced and the search was continuing. The Acting Chairman was Warfield T. Firor. He was a Hopkins alumnus, a member of Phi Chi, an excellent surgeon, with a kindly, low key, but forceful, personality.

Dick Shakleford was his first assistant. The usual surgical resident training was eight to ten years, as one worked up the ladder. In his final year, he operated on all the professor's ward patients, 8 to 12 daily, usually without supervision by any surgical faculty. I remember Sloan, Jonas and Longmire, but few others. It was in this trimester that I obtained Dr. Rich's approval of my questionnaire and mailed it to the deans of all the medical schools in the United States. Returns began to come in during the spring and final trimester of the year. We also worked in The Huntarian (Austin Lamont) Laboratory.

While our group was in the surgical trimester, one of my classmate friends, Robert Allen, told me he was hoping to get a surgical internship at a private Baltimore hospital, the Union Memorial, after graduation. He wanted to serve there as a clinical clerk the coming summer so he would be known to the Surgical Intern Selection Committee. Bob was from Rockland, Maine. The previous summer he had tutored the three sons of the Williams family from Baltimore. Their "camp" was at Small Point on the Atlantic south of Bath, the home of the boat building Sewalls for 200 years. Bob asked if I would be interested in such a summer job. My reply was that I had to check with my parents, because the job did not give much pay other than room and board. Happily, my family approved. We met the Williams parents and they offered me the job which is how I came to spend the summer of 1940 at Small Point, Maine.

The final trimester of that year was on the gynecological and obstetric wards; observing home deliveries in East Baltimore, and getting exposure to geriatric and demented patients in the Baltimore City Hospital. It was far enough away from N. Broadway that it required a ride, since public transportation was complicated. Our classmate, Frank Hinman, from San Francisco, had a car and he provided me transportation, not only in year 3, but in year 4 as well. He also gave me the idea of spending my 4th year "free" trimester at Harvard as a clinical clerk on the Peter Bent Brigham service of Professor Soma Weiss.

A boarder at 1013 was Robert W. Wilkins, MD. He was a graduate of Harvard Medical School, interned at Boston City

Hospital, and was on the research team of Soma Weiss, one of the earliest Clinical Pharmacologists. I told Wilkins that I had a classmate who was going to spend the summer as a clinical clerk with Weiss, then Medicine Department Chair. I asked weather Wilkins would recommend me for such a clerkship in the second trimester of my fourth year. Wilkins did, and I was accepted for 1 November, 1940.

I should mention now a major episode in my life. That was the advice given to me in several conversations over a period of time by Ludwig Eichna, MD, who was with me at 1013 for three years. This particular episode occurred in the early spring of 1940. Ike's postgraduate work at Hopkins was a result of early success at the Hospital of the University of Pennsylvania, where he finished as the Chief Resident in Medicine. This led to his being given a fellowship at Hopkins Hospital. Thus, Ike knew well how the Penn Internship and Medical Residency system worked. By law in the state of Pennsylvania, a medical graduate had to have a two year rotating internship in order to apply to take the State Board Licensing Examinations. Only after you passed these Boards could you be licensed to practice.

At the end of the third year, I was aware of how little I knew about the practical aspects of the several specialties, and I was attracted more to the rotating internship rather than the "straight" of Hopkins and Maryland Hospitals. I had the hunch that I would be a better internist, and, hopefully, a specialist in cardiovascular disease management, if I had a "hands on" experience in a teaching hospital. I.e.: "watch one, teach one, do one, master many." Eichna alerted me to the system by which interns were chosen by William Pepper, Dean of the School of Medicine for the HUP 2 year rotating service. The Chairman of the Department of Medicine was his younger brother, Perry Pepper. Their father, also an MD, had not only been the Dean, but was also the Provost of the University. It was in his provost period that the Senior William Pepper raised the money (in 1875) to build and open the first teaching University Hospital in the USA. Ike said that every year, Dean Pepper would invite his Dean friends to recommend a graduate for the Penn Internship so that there would be, as it was in 1941, 24 Penn graduates, and 3 from other schools. What I did not know then, nor did Eichna, was that the most recent Hopkins graduate to intern at HUP was Jonathan Rhoads, MD, Hopkins '32. Eichna suggested that I approach the Hopkins Dean, Alan Chesney, to find out what my standing in the 1941 class might be. Was I rated high enough to be recommended by Dr. Chesney if Penn would invite Hopkins to send a '41 graduate? Dr. Chesney was very cordial. He said that I was the first one of my class to consult him about an HUP internship, but he was vague about when he last had an opportunity to recommend a student to Penn. He said he would have to look up my course record and talk to some of my third year clinical teachers before he could give me an answer.

I suggested several faculty members who knew me personally, such as Dr. Rich and Dr. Follis of the Pathology Department, as well as Dr. Longcope. Not long afterwards, I received a letter from Dean Chesney stating that he would be able to recommend me to Dean Pepper at Penn if a 1941 graduate was to be invited. Ike, on learning this, said: "Now you have to go to Penn and meet Dean Pepper and tell him you want to intern at HUP." This was in early April 1940 and I already agreed with Mrs. Williams that I would drive one of their cars to the Fay School in Massachusetts and pick up the two youngest, Sewall and Arthur, before going on to Small Point. I ruled out a June visit to Dean Pepper and decided I would go soon, perhaps the next weekend. My parents had sent me money for the train. Dean Chesney had written to Dean Pepper and asked for a specific appointment date for me to visit HUP. A reply was received within a week, and I arranged to go there for a Saturday visit in the third week of April, 1940.

I went to the Dean's office at Penn and had a very pleasant interview with William Pepper, MD. Upon learning that I was leaning toward a Medical residency and a career in Internal Medicine, he called his brother, O.H. Perry Pepper and walked me over to the hospital where I met the Chairman of Medicine. When he heard that I was going to spend the summer in Maine, tutoring three brothers, 16,15, and 14, he chuckled and wished me good luck. Within the hour I was on a train back to Baltimore and feeling optimistic about my career.

In a week or so, Dr. Chesney called me into his office and told me he was formally responding to Dr. Pepper's invitation to recommend me for the two year rotating internship at HUP beginning 25 June 1941. So, before I left for Maine in June 1940, I knew where I was going to be for my fourth year "free quarter" a well as my internship. I left Baltimore in the Williams' car in late May, and stopped in Boston where I had arranged to meet Joseph Lutz Flynn. He had completed his first year in Harvard Business School and was preparing to return to Youngstown for the summer. I also contacted Don Gribbon in Boston. He had finished his second year at Harvard Law School and had been elected to the Law Review. He was also chosen to preside over the "moot court" project. When he learned I was to be at Brigham Hospital for a fourth year program in Medicine, he said he would get me a ticket for the "moot court" sometime after my arrival there on 1ˢᵗ November. At this time we arranged that I would drive back with Flynn and Dan to Youngstown for the 1940 Christmas vacation. I also made some contacts at Harvard concerning where I might live in the three months I would be clerking at the Brigham Hospital with Professor Weiss.

I picked up the Williams brothers at the Fay School and it was a seven hour drive from Boston to Bath. They knew the directions from Bath to Small Point and we arrived in the pouring rain which continued for most of the month of June. Already in the "camp", a house with 8 bedrooms and 4 baths, was "Icy", the cook, her son, who was the major "heavy-lifter"

Small Point 1940

and an upstairs maid, a quiet older woman. The mother, father, younger sister Anne, age 6, and the older brother Jack, age 16, (in his second year at Hill School), had not arrived as yet.

Sewall and Arthur's teachers had provided them with an outline of what was to be covered during the summer. We started immediately, having a session after breakfast for two hours each morning, five days a week. On their own, they were to study a book from their outline for a half hour. In the class following that reading, I would ask each to tell me what they read and then I would question them about the details for another half hour. We would cover two other subjects in the remaining time. Later in the month Jack arrived. His project was to prepare for his first try at the College Boards. His father, a travel agent in Baltimore, had been to Yale, and that was where Jack hoped to go. Unfortunately he was a poor student!

Their camp was a large house, situated on a rise about ¼ mile inland from the Atlantic beach. The community was on a "point"; a small peninsula with Casco Bay on the inland side. The weather was cold, and the cook's son had the chore of getting the firewood and keeping the fireplaces, two on each side of the ground floor, lit in the early morning. The island looking to the east was Sequin, one of the major Maine lighthouses along its rocky coast.

After the bookwork, the younger brothers showed me where the docks were, where the "Small Point special" sailboats (designed by Sterling Burgess and built at the Bath Iron Works boatyard in 1938), were kept, and where the tennis courts were situated,

Williams Family at Small Point

as brother Jack was said to be one of the best tennis players in the colony. I was also shown the houses of the other family members as well as the year-round general store. The proprietor, Ray McIntyre, told us there would be no Cokes this year since they sold too fast and "were too much trouble to keep in supply." He was a retired lobsterman who skippered the Commodore's boat for the twice-weekly sailing races. Mrs. Williams' first cousin, Sumner Sewall, was then the Governor of Maine, and he had a house there with his second wife. One of Mrs. Lani Sewall Williams' brothers, Sag, had a house, wife and young children there. Her older brother, Harold Marsh Sewall, had the family house in Bath, (now the main building in the Maine Maritime Museum), but did not have a house in Small Point. Lani was born in Hawaii, when her father was the American representative there before the whites took over in the 1890's. Mrs. Williams' younger sister, Camilla Sewall Edge, was married to Walter Edge, a self-made advertising wizard from Atlantic City. He left business early to go into politics. Camilla was his second wife, and he had a son by his late wife, who was his namesake. Edge was currently the Governor of New Jersey, having been the Governor before he was the U.S. Ambassador to France. The first cousins were Loyal, Camilla and Mary Esther. The Edge and Sewall men were all Republicans and they had been in Philadelphia to help secure the nomination for their man, Wendell Wilkie. Some antiwar Republicans wanted to nominate the famous Trans Atlantic flier Charles Lindbergh. He was too anti-Semitic for the power brokers of the party at that time. So it was "Win with Wilkie!"

Small Point was essentially Sewall property. The grand dame of the colony was Mrs. Arthur Sewall, whose son was a Bath broker with two children; Mary, Smith '39, and William, MIT '49. Most of the summer visitors came about the weekend before the 4th of July, and there was an active social life with "Win with Wilkie" and "Bundles for Britain" gatherings. After the 4th, most of the men, including the cook's son, left the families to return to their jobs; but entertaining took place every day in the afternoon and evening. I was pressed into service as a bartender, although I knew nothing about wine, liquor, beer or mixed drinks. Lani Sewall Williams, a charming woman, tutored me on my bartending.

Johnny Williams was the principal in the Raymond Whitcomb Baltimore travel agency and returned to be with us at Small Point on a few weekends. His mother had a house at York, Maine, and his brother, an artist, Arthur Foster Williams, stayed there with her. On one occasion, at Lani's suggestions, I drove the two younger brothers to York Harbor for a weekend with their grandmother. She was a kind Baltimore woman, and arranged for me to have tickets to see John Barrymore and his daughter on the stage at a tent playhouse that weekend in Ogunquit.

One of the non Sewall families there had the best tennis court. That was the Ted Curtis family of Rochester, New York. He was an official of the Eastman Kodak Company. He was there that summer because he was a friend of Sumner Sewall, the Governor. Ted and Sumner had been airmen in France in World War I and served in the Eddie Rickenbacker "Hat in the Ring" squadron. Like Eddie, these two were also aces, having been credited with shooting down five German planes each. Ted and his wife Agnes were enthusiastic tennis players. Jack and I were often called to join them in a two set match. We played them well, particularly on Jack's serve, but we never could beat them at both sets. Perhaps that was why we received so many invitations.

Tennis at Small Point

Jack was better coordinated, a natural athlete, and in dress, a bit of a "dandy." He put little effort into his studies. Sewall was the most serious. He was also a good worker and helped the staff in any way that he could. He was particularly kind and affectionate to his six year old sister, Anne. Arthur was the most fun-loving, much like his mother Lani. He was also as handsome as his mother was beautiful.

Activities were family oriented, with beach clambakes, lobster lunches or dinners, weekly sailing races, and swimming in the Atlantic Ocean and Casco Bay. On Friday nights, we drove about 50 miles to Boothbay Harbor in two cars with at least ten of the cousins. There was an open air dance floor with music and a band of young musicians. The cousins danced with each other. There was no smoking or drinking of either soft drinks or alcohol. We would be back at Small Point before midnight.

John Williams came up for Labor Day weekend. He was kind to me, and it was at that time that he thanked me and gave me an envelope with $220. That was $20 more than I thought I was going to be paid. I had met cousin Mary Sewall Smith '39, daughter of the Bath broker Arthur Sewall, because of the thoughtfulness of

Lani. She gave me one night off each week and provided me with one of the family cars. It was on one of those occasions that Lani arranged for me to have a date with Mary Sewall. I liked Mary. She was very intelligent, fun-loving, had many friends, and was a good dancer. In late August, she told me that, although she was uncertain about her graduate school work at Boston University Social Service Studies, she had been able to arrange for an apartment, and was going to see if she could finish with a Master's Degree in the coming academic year. When she was told that I would be at the Brigham Hospital for three months as of 1 Nov. 1940, she allowed that she would like me to call her when I came.

Mary Sewall

Walking to the hospital on the first day of classes, I had a great feeling of relaxation and a joyous sense of expectation. During the previous three years I was confident, but tense and uneasy. By September 1940, I was at ease and in good physical condition. I knew where and, with whom, I would be studying during my "free quarter" in Boston. Also, I knew where I would be doing my internship, but this I kept to myself. Thus my fourth year was going to be less pressured than that of most of my classmates. The first trimester courses were Outpatient Medicine and Surgery. This meant that one reported to the hospital Outpatient Department before the first patient's appointment and the instructor assigned you the waiting patient. I was comfortable with those encounters, being certain that I was going to be able to comfort that individual and relieve pain even when I could not cure. The essence of this was to be a good listener and a careful examiner. When I was certain that I understood what the patient expected to gain from their visit, I would excuse myself, and leave the patient in the examining room so I could find the instructor. Then I would present the facts and suggest the management. When he or she agreed, the process would be implemented. Most times, before the patient departed, and with the student, the instructor would visit briefly with the patient, making certain that the patient's best interests were being served. The procedure was the same for Surgery, Gynecology, Pediatrics and Psychiatry. At that stage in our training, it was "showing up" and being kind in doing what needed to be done. There was little to be learned from the "how to" books. Our teachers taught by example.

Early in the trimester there was a notice on the bulletin board of the Dean's Office. Dr. Howard Kelly, one of the Hopkins "big four," was about to dispose of his books and other items in his library, and the Hopkins Medical School students were to have the first choices. A list was available, and his representative was to be in the Administration Building on certain days and times. I was busy selling microscopes and helping Phi Chi with rushing. I realized that the Kelly collection had to be studied. On the list was a book, "Cushing's Life of William Osler," that I had chanced upon as a high school student at the Belmont Avenue Branch of Youngstown's Carnegie Library. This was a two-volume edition, and I had read it avidly. This was in the back of my mind, when, I had made John Hopkins my first choice. Cushing had met Osler when they were both at Hopkins in the decade after the Hopkins Hospital opened in 1889. Later, Cushing went to Harvard Medical School and performed neurosurgery at the Peter Bent Brigham Hospital in Boston.

I contacted Dr. Kelly's representative and said I would like to have Dr. Kelly's two volume edition of Cushing's Osler. I agreed to pay the asking price. Not more than a week went by when I learned that I had obtained the two volume edition. Knowing that Osler and Kelly had been at Penn at the same time in the 1880s, I had an idea. I suggested to Kelly's man that I was going to Penn for my internship, and that it would mean much to me to have Dr. Kelly inscribe the book appropriately which he did. When our son Tom was awarded his certificate by the American Board of Internal Medicine, I presented him with this highly valued set. My classmate and fellow Phi Chi brother, Willard Goodwin, the nephew of a prominent California Urologist, and an authority on the History of Medicine, also wanted Cushing's Osler. Although disappointed, he bid on, and won, the collection of letters that Kelly had received from Osler and Cushing. Goodwin wrote an article about the interaction between these early Hopkins icon which was published a year later in the Johns Hopkins Bulletin of the History of Medicine. It was edited by one of our prominent teachers, Henry Sigerist.

My analysis of the procedures for early TB case finding in the Medical Schools that responded had been edited by Dr. Rich. I submitted it to the National Association of Medical Students and it was published in their Journal the next year. We had an active group of this association at Hopkins. During a meeting of the program group, the suggestion was made that another viewpoint of abortion and medical ethics might be desirable. Father T.V. Moore was an MD, and had been a graduate student of Adolf Meyer in his specialty-Psychiatry. I invited him to Hopkins to talk on "Abortion and Medical Ethics" and he accepted. The largest auditorium in the hospital was reserved for a date in the spring trimester. The lecture was a great success and attracted a large crowd.

The Harvard Dean, Dr. Hale, and his assistant, Miss Murphy, helped me to arrange for room and board at the home of a widow, a five minute walk from the Brigham. My premed classmates, Benditt and Fowler, both of whom had won full scholarships, were in fourth year classes at other hospitals such as Boston City and the Mass. General. Most of my work was at the Brigham, but I did attend lectures by Harvard faculty at the McLean (Psychiatry) and the Deaconess, where Professor Joslin was the diabetes expert. Ward Fowler had married a 1937 classmate, Joan Kelley, and they invited me to dinner at their apartment. Joan's sister was there, attending Radcliffe, having transferred after one year at Swarthmore. Anita later married our '37 classmate, Oliver Payne Pearson, and they lived in Orinda where he was a Professor of Biology at UC Berkley. They were one of the first families the Hafkenschiels visited when we moved to California in 1965.

Soma Weiss was a charismatic individual and quite a showman. On Saturday mornings he put on a clinic for the local practitioners where he highlighted the fourth year students. He had gathered a strong group of young professors and housestaff including Stead, Kunkel, Warren, Myers, Hickok, and Janeway, many of whom went on to Chairmen Departments of Medicine. What was different, was that at Harvard, the fourth year students were doing ward work, as

Hopkins students did in the third year. So this was another "hands on" experience caring for sickbed patients under the supervision of excellent instructors. One student, John Farmer, did a memorable job in tracing down the causative organism of an infected animal (rat?) bite sustained by a young black woman living in a lower class apartment dwelling. She had an acute febrile illness with an unusual skin rash. Later, his report was published in the New England Journal of Medicine.

I was helped considerably in seeing the sights of Boston by my new girlfriend, Mary Sewall, whom I met through the good works of Lani Sewall Williams. She was Lani's cousin, whose father was "the banker" in Bath, as well as Chairman of the Board of the Bath Hospital. He was a graduate of Harvard, and was the most intellectual of all the Sewall men I met the summer before. Mary had a car and an apartment on Commonwealth Avenue. Her classes were at Boston University. As a social worker in training, she had to visit settlement houses in the less affluent areas of Boston. She introduced me to concerts at Symphony Hall, historic places, and well known Boston restaurants. On one occasion we went to a Harvard basketball game. The coach at that time was Wesley Fesler, a former All-American end at Ohio State in the early 1930s. Dan Gribbon invited me to attend the "moot court" program which he chaired in his last year at Harvard Law School. He was also the Vice Chairman of the Law Review that year. On Christmas vacation Joseph Lutz Flynn drove Dan and me to Youngstown and then back to Boston.

In January 1941 I was invited out to dinner at the Harvard Faculty Club by Robert Wilkins, who had been made a professor at Boston University School of Medicine. He told me he was going to be married to Peggy at Newburyport the next August and asked me to be in his wedding party. He introduced me to Paul Kunkel and Eugene Stead whom he worked with at Boston City Hospital Thorndike Laboratory when the Chief was Soma Weiss. Kunkel and five other MDs were dinner guests of a widow who had a big house and put on a great dinner. I had a pleasant evening as the dinner guest of Charles Janeway and his wife who was the sister of Mary Bradley. Mary was living on North Broadway across from 1013, and I met her walking to the hospital, where she was a post graduate Bacteriology student. She introduced me to her roommate, Mary Wick of Youngstown, the daughter of Myron Wick, a banker friend of my mother's. The two Marys and Eugene Meyer IV, one of my closest friends, double dated. "Bill", as Meyer was called, later married Mary Bradley. Mary Wick also married a Hopkins medical graduate. Before I returned to Baltimore, Mary Sewall asked me if I would spend a long weekend at her home in Bath which I did, and was happy to meet her mother, father, and brother Bill. When I was at MIT in 1948 in the Graduate School, I saw Bill again. Leaving Boston, I said goodbye to Mary. But it was not a surprise to me that she encouraged me to be with Bob and Peggy when they married in August.

Professor Adolph Meyer was retiring. "Bill" Meyer, Jacques, Gruenberg and I arranged to have a gift for the Professor which we presented to him when he invited us to his home. He was moved, and we were thrilled that we had done it.

There was a Phi Chi dance that was a happy occasion with lasting benefits. Billy Higgins had a date with Patsy Crooks, who was his sister's roommate at a school in New York City. They were both to be in Palo Alto and Menlo Park when we moved to California in 1965. Also, I met A. M. Harvey and Calvin Kay, both of whom I would play golf with years later. It was Robert Wilkins who introduced me to A. M. Harvey, M. D. "Mac" was a native of Little Rock and a graduate of Washington and Lee, as well as Hopkins. After an Osler internship and residency, he had spent a postgraduate year in London at a Neurological Institute, where he had met Wilkins. On his return to the U. S., Harvey wanted to learn more about medical instrumentation, and he arranged with Detlev Bronk to spend a year in the Biophysics Department of the Medical School at Penn. Dr. Harvey then became the Senior Resident in Medicine at Hopkins. After our fourth year, he accepted a Professorship at Vanderbilt. He was there until the Hopkins General Hospital was activated after Pearl Harbor. After his military service, he became the Osler Professor of Medicine, Chairman of the Department, at Hopkins. As he was beginning his year as Chief Resident, he told me that he ha been disappointed with the Department of Medicine at Penn. This did not change my mind, being in the last month of medical school. My mother and father took the train to Baltimore to be present at my graduation.

Dr. Charles Austrian was the best Pulmonary Specialist in Baltimore. Because of my father's chronic cough, I asked Dr. Austrian whether he would examine my father after graduation. He agreed, and I was with them as Dr. Austrian made a careful physical examination as well as a chest fluoroscopy and x-ray. The results were negative and I was reassured.

Mary Sewall also came to my graduation, and, because of the favorable results of my father's physical examination, we had a celebration lunch at Miller's, the best seafood eatery in Baltimore at that time. Then we put my parents on the train to Youngstown and Mary drove me back to 1013. I wanted to pack my few belongings, other than clothes, in an extra suitcase to store at HUP. Mary said she would drive me there. On the way to Philadelphia, Mary told me she was going to wait for me to drop off some of my load at the HUP and told me her plan. She knew that I was not to start at HUP until 21 June and she had arranged with her mother and father for me to be their house guest until I had to leave for Philadelphia. Her father cooperated with the plan, taking me to interesting sights in Bath as well as a tour of the Bath Hospital. I spent one morning with him at his work in the bank, and then he took me to lunch at his club. Mary's mother and brother, Bill, were just as kind. I told Mary the date of Bob Wilkins' weekend marriage to Peggy in Newburyport. She said she would be there. At the end of my visit I booked a place on the Bar Harbor Express train from Bath to Philadelphia.

4. Internship and Marriage: 1941-2

Dr. Hatch, the Internship Director, greeted the first year interns and gave them a sheet which showed what services they were to be on for the first six months. On this sheet were the names of the second year interns and the names of the Assistant Residents who were the House Staff leaders on any given ward. The representatives of O.H. Perry Pepper were the Senior Attending and the Junior Attending. They were members of the volunteer faculty in the sense that one volunteered for a specific month he would take the duty in a given calendar year. Dr. Pepper also assigned a faculty member to each ward whose responsibility was to supervise the eight students assigned to the 32 bed ward. The hospital was built in 1875 and was located on Spruce Street, in the block between 36th and 34th Streets in the center of the University Campus in West Philadelphia.

The routine was much the same as at Hopkins. There were only two interns assigned to a 32 bed ward; one first year intern, (I was that on ward D, a men's ward, on the second floor of the hospital.) My fellow second year intern was John Thomas of Texas. The students were to do the complete history and physical examination after the intern did a brief exam, so that he could write an admission note and orders. Dr. Henry Hopkins was the faculty member who supervised the

Godparents of Richard Conroy

students, reviewed their write ups, and discussed management with them. One difference from Hopkins was that the interns presented the facts to the Attending on the morning rounds of house staff (business rounds). Some medical students might also be present but they were scheduled each day for rounds with Dr. Hopkins and the Assistant Resident/teaching rounds.

Grand Rounds were held once weekly in a large lecture room called Alumni Hall, and were presided over by the Chairman, O.H. Pepper. The cases to be presented were usually selected by Dr. Hopkins and the teaching assistant resident. My assignment was for July and August on ward D, and September and October on the female ward B. Later I had several weeks on Pepper. The residents were John Helms and John Sayen, and the second year intern, Charles Merckel, served on ward B with me. He was also my roommate, and a charming, jocular, hard-working man who had gone to Wayne University Medical School in Detroit. We became life-long friends.

The Chairman of Surgery was I. S. Ravdin, an alumnus of Penn, '18, and a member of the Penn Chapter, Phi Chi Medical Fraternity, who was from Indiana. When I was an intern there was another Surgical service chaired by Dr. Eldridge Eliason. For November and December I was assigned to the Ravdin Service. With the Pearl Harbor disaster on 7 Dec. 1941, and the immediate declaration of war, the 2 year rotating internship was shortened to one year. Thus, for the next 6 to 7 months, the medical and surgical assignments were halved, and services such as General Surgery, Neurosurgery, Obstetrics, Pediatrics, X-Ray and Clinical Laboratory were all moved up into the remaining months of the one year program ending 30 June 1942.

X-ray began in July. It was the job of the intern to hand-deliver his requests to a secretary/technician in the basement X-Ray Department each morning. This was to ensure that the patients whose x-rays were most urgent would be scheduled as soon as possible. On my second day on X-ray duty, I secured the forms, and filled out the requests as I thought indicated. I took at least eight of my sixteen patients for study that day. When I presented these to the attractive young woman in a white uniform, She told that the requests did not show the urgency of the procedure, possible diagnosis, etc. This meant I had to rewrite most of them under her tutelage. She was patient, but I came away feeling she was unduly rigorous. She looked familiar to me, but was not wearing a name tag. I left there feeling chastened. When I went to my room that evening after a long, tiring day, I asked Charley Merckel if he knew who this woman might be. He said he didn't but that all of the staffs names, addresses, and phone numbers could be found on a bulletin board in one of the department corridors.

In the next two or three days, I found the bulletin board and looked over the names. There was a name on there that I remember seeing in the Swarthmore College Bulletin in 1933-1934. That was how I first met Lucinda Buchanan Thomas in the X-Ray Department in July 1941. She had graduated from Swarthmore in 1934 and this was her third year working in the X-Ray Department.

My assignment to the Pediatrics Ward in January 1942 was with Dr. Franklin Murphy. He was a Penn '41 graduate and one of the three married interns in our group of 27. He was originally from Kansas, the son of a prominent physician . He had part of his college and Medical School training at Oxford. His wife, Judy, was very attractive and had been his high school sweetheart. Murphy liked to talk and loved a female audience. The assistant resident in Pediatrics was a woman M.D. After we had breakfast together in the doctor's dining room, we walked to Ward K together. Murphy would go

Lucy Thomas

to the nurse's office where the resident, Dr. Cross, and the nurses were working on the charts. Murphy would talk. I would go onto the floor, where most of the nurses were caring for their patients. When I saw a nurse not busy with a patient, I would ask her to show me the sickest child on the floor, and ask her to explain to me how they were caring for this individual. As the month went on, there seemed to be fewer nurses on floor duty. I learned that those who were not married and did not have a 'steady' were signing up to be second lieutenants in the Army Nurse Corps. One morning, I saw a new face, a beautiful woman in a Red Cross Nurse's Aid uniform. She appeared to be caring for the healthy newborns. I told one of the nurses I knew that I wanted to be introduced which is how I met Carol MacDonald Smith in January, 1942.

Soon after Pearl Harbor, the HUP-20th General Hospital was placed on active duty as of 1 May 1942. Dr. I.S. Ravdin was the Hospital Director, and many of the medical faculty had already signed up at his request. It was announced that only second year interns would be accepted for duty with that group.

In February or March, when I was doing intern duty on less intense assignments such as X-Ray and Clinical Laboratory, I decided to serve, but was unsure which branch I should join? My reasoning was: I was healthy, had a great education, great family support, and that I was a citizen of a great country. My family had been unusually supportive of what I thought were good opportunities and I was eager to start repaying them for their sacrifices. Some of my fellow interns were thinking of the Navy, but I did not think that my experience on "Small Point Specials" in the summer of 1940 was anything that would recommend me. On my hours off I was spending time in the Biophysics Department, headed by Detlev Bronk, PhD, Swarthmore '21. He had recruited me for government instrument studies which ultimately led to the development of the oximeter. One day when I was there serving as a subject, Professor Bronk came into the room. He had been in Washington for several days and had asked the Air Surgeon to consider-the training of airmen by aviation physiologists, MDs and PhDs. He asked me whether I was considering military service. I told him that I had done the preliminary work to join the Army Medical Corps, but had not yet been accepted for a physical examination. He then gave me a "pep" talk, saying that when I received my commission, I was the MD type he needed for his aviation physiologist program. When I received my commission and orders, he wanted to discuss the project further and guide me if I wanted to join that group. I passed the physical, was commissioned 1st LT, and was told to report to Carlisle Barracks, Pa on 1 August 1942. Bronk advised me how to complete the specific Army forms.

I had little time off for dates, and spending money was minimal, receiving a dollar each week in the letter my mother and father sent me. I had a date with Lucinda in December, when we went to the Penn-Swarthmore basketball game at the Palestra. We went dancing afterwards, and, inasmuch as she was still in training at HUP X-Ray Department, she arranged for me to stay overnight at her grandmother Stackhouse's house at 240 Tulpehocken, Germantown. There were dates with Carol in which I used public transportation to get to her mother's house on Lesley Road, Villanova. I would stay overnight and, after breakfast, Carol, her stepfather, and I rode public transportation into town, and Carol and I would walk from the 36th Street elevated to HUP. Carol asked me to go to a circus on a Friday afternoon when I was able to be free, which I did and enjoyed. Her next invitation was a daytime canoeing trip on the Brandywine with several other couples. This I had to decline because I was on duty.

I had few dates with Lucinda between December and April, as I had little money and even less free time. We met one day in the X-Ray Department and she asked me what I was planning to do. I told her and she responded by saying that her graduation from X-Ray was 30 April and she had been offered a job at Jeanes Hospital, a Quaker facility in N. Philadelphia, and she was going to start 1 May. I told her I had my commission and was going on active duty, 1 August 1942. My plan was to take the State Medical Boards sometime in late June or early July. We made a date to go to Valley Forge in late April to see the spring foliage and have dinner at a place in the great valley where her Thomas family had been Welch Quaker farmers since the 1780's. This we did, and it left me thinking how I might be able to keep in touch with Lucinda. She told me she would be 30 on May 11, 1942. Carol was then 21. Lucinda was not interested in getting married, even though I had never brought up the subject, inasmuch as I was going on active duty in the near future.

The last several weeks of our duty, one of our group of first-year men, Tom Gucker, was given the responsibilities of Dr. Hatch. Tom was a Princeton and Penn Med. Alumnus and -had been badly crippled by Polio. Because of this he was not eligible for the military. He coordinated our final days by arranging that each would have a key and a cash bonus as well as a Certificate of Diploma. This was unexpected and left us with a good feeling. Several of the intern group who wished to have the hospital provide room and board for the 4-5 days of the exam, had put in writing a request for a place to stay during the exams. Tom Gucker had arranged the accommodations for three of the four of us whose homes were out of state. Before the exams started, I went out to Youngstown and my parents allowed me to drive their car back to Philadelphia so I would have a car during exams. My plan was to return to Youngstown after the exams until August 1,1942 when I went on active duty. Having the car, I contacted Lucinda and asked her out for a date. We went out to dinner at a restaurant and then to a movie in Germantown before returning her to her grandmother's house. At that time, she asked whether I was going to be around for the 4th of July, as she had been asked by her cousins to go with them on a family picnic at her cousin, Sam Pennypacker's farm in Schwenksville. I told her I would ask Tom Gucker whether I could stay after the exams over the 4th of July. Tom agreed, and I alerted Lucinda that I would join her and her cousins at the picnic.I contacted my parents and told them my stay in Philadelphia was to be extended. I later learned that they were surprised that I was interested in a Philadelphia woman rather than Mary from Maine. I completed the exams and left my parent's address for notification of my exam results. Later, my mother phoned me that I had passed and that I was now licensed to practice in Pennsylvania. Another hurdle had been jumped.

Aubrey Pennypacker, Lucy, Powell, Lucy Stackhouse, Ben

The picnic on the fourth was my first opportunity to meet Lucinda's cousins. She had two brothers, Ben and Powell and two half brothers, Rhys and Bill from her father's second marriage. I had met her younger brother, Powell, a reporter for the Bulletin who had gone to George School and Gettysburg College. He was currently in Officer's training at Fort Lee, Virginia. Her older brother, Ben, was married with young children and was living in Delaware County and working at Westinghouse. At that time I did not know her half brothers . Her father, B.A. Thomas, Swarthmore,

1899, and Penn Med. '02, was a Philadelphia Urologist until he died in May, 1930, just after Lucinda finished at Friend's Central School. Her mother, Lucy Buchanan Stackhouse, married B.A. Thomas in 1907, and died in the flu epidemic in 1918. At the time Lucy was living with her grandmother, Lucy Buchanan Stackhouse whose late husband, Powell Stackhouse, had died in 1927. Lucinda's grandmother was his fourth wife, and was a niece of his first wife. His first three wives had died, or drowned in the Johnstown Flood. Thus, there were cousins down from the sons and daughters of Powell's four marriages. Lucinda had only one aunt, Katherine Stackhouse. She had married B.A. Pennypacker, and they had only one son, Sam Pennypacker, II. It was on his farm that the picnic was to be held. The other cousins were the MacCallas of Wynnewood and the Chalfants of West Chester. Most of the other cousins were living in the Johnstown and Pittsburgh areas.

The 4th of July was a beautiful day, and I met Lucinda and Gertrude and Powell MacCalla at 240 Tulpehocken, her grandmother's house. We then drove in the MacCalla's car to Schwenksville, (Pennypacker's Mills), where we met Margaret and Sam. They had prepared most of the food, and as

Pennypacker Mills

we were leaving for the picnic site on the creek that flowed through their acres, we learned that the Chalfants would not be able to join us. The gathering was very pleasant, mostly eating, drinking and conversation. I was trying to learn how this group of young people fit in with the cousins who were not present (but were talked about). At that time Lucinda had started working at Jeanes Hospital, and there was much questioning of what she was doing and how she liked it. I learned that, although the grandparents of Stackhouse and Thomas were Quakers, Lucinda and her brothers were raised as Presbyterians, and that, only recently, had Lucinda and her brother, Powell, joined the Quakers at the Green Street Meeting. They were "convinced" Friends. When the sun set, we moved to the house and had coffee and dessert before starting back to Germantown.

We arrived at 240 Tulpehocken about 9 P.M. Lucinda's grandmother's physician was awaiting her return. The MacCallas had left for their home across the river in Wynnewood. The doctor said, "Lucinda, I don't think your grandmother will live through the night. I will be back here at 7 A.M." I returned to HUP. When I called the next morning Lucinda told me that her grandmother had died during the night. She asked me if I would come out later in the day and be prepared to stay at 240 as she had arranged with her Uncle Aubrey Pennypacker. I later learned that he, a Philadelphia lawyer, was the executor of the Stackhouse Estate. The specific reason for this invitation was for me to meet her cousins who would be arriving later in the day. I agreed, and packed up my belongings at HUP, said goodbye to Tom Gucker, and drove out to 240. We were alone when I arrived, except for the staff, who were preparing food and drinks pending the arrival of members of the family. This was when I proposed to Lucinda that she should marry me before I would go on active duty. She did not seem surprised, but indicated that she would have to think it over and would let me know in a day or so. Soon her older brother arrived with his wife, her younger brother, Powell, was on leave, and, from Johnstown, PA, came the older son of Powell Stackhouse, Daniel Stackhouse, with his daughter, Kitty.

The next day Lucinda said she would like to be married on 18 July. Her cousin, Powell MacCalla, had already volunteered to make reservations for a hotel room for our honeymoon. Her uncle Aubrey had said that we could stay at 240 until July 31st, when he was going to start settling the Stackhouse Estate, putting the house and contents up

Powell MacCalla

for sale. Lucinda also mentioned that she had been offered a higher-paying x-ray job at Bryn Mawr Hospital because of a situation there that had been worked out by the Chief of X-ray and her former boss, the Chief of X-ray at Penn, Eugene Pendergrass. Uncle Aubrey said Lucinda might stay at his home on 6626 MacCallum Street as long as she needed. My mother and father accepted the invitation to stay at 240 and, together with Lucinda's brothers, we were married at St. Sophie's Church in Germantown on 18 July. The reception, arranged by Uncle Aubrey and his wife, Mary Ferguson, was at 240 Tulpehocken. My mother and father drove back to Youngstown in their car. Lucinda and I drove to the Cavalier Hotel in Virginia Beach in her car and had a great time until July 28th, when we returned to 240 Tulpehocken.

Just Married

5. Military Service: 1942-45

Early on 1 August Lucinda and I left the home of Uncle Aubrey Pennypacker at 6636 MacCallum Street in Germantown. Lucinda drove me to the Medical Field Service School in Carlisle. We learned that I would be free to leave on 31 August with new orders and she said she would meet me and drive me where ordered.

I, like many of the officers as 1st Lt. Medical Corps of the Army of the United States (AUS), was reporting for duty in the military for the first time. In the four weeks that followed most of the men were classified as Medical Officer, General Duty. We slept in barracks and ate in the same mess hall. We all had the same uniform: summer khakis. Our day started with calisthenics, then breakfast, and after that, lectures until noon. After lunch there were field excursions and some approaches to first aid on a simulated battlefield.

The most impressive of the lecturers was a medical officer with a German name and accent who was particularly skilled in presenting the problems faced by a medical officer in the war zone situation. There were individual interviews early in the first week. Each of us filled out a form summarizing our background, interests, and top two choices for service. After the forms were completed and submitted for review, an officer met with each individual and asked why he had stated his first choice. This was my opportunity to present my knowledge of the Air Corps Altitude Training Program and my desire to be qualified as an Aviation Physiologist as well as a Medical Officer General Duty.

I recall two other Medicos. One, a fellow intern, was named Camillo DeBernadinis. The other was Herman Hellerstein of Cleveland, who became a Cardiologist. Graduation day was August 31st, 1942 which was highlighted by the awarding of a certificate and a copy of orders for our next assignment. My orders were to report to an Air Corps Station which I took as a good sign.

Lucinda was enjoying her work at Bryn Mawr Hospital. She was a very efficient person and I knew she was helping Aubrey Pennypacker as best she could. Aubrey (who treated Lucinda like she were his daughter and the sister of his only son, Sam Pennypacker

II), had arranged for Lucinda to store her most prized possessions, such as the portrait of her Aunt Josephine, on his third floor. The plan was for her to load her car and meet me on the last day of the Carlisle training. Lucinda arrived in her '34 Ford convertible with her possessions and I showed her my orders to Bowman Field, Louisville, Kentucky. We called my parents and said we would be stopping in Youngstown. We spent the first night of our military life at the 360 Fairgreen home of my parents. It was their second meeting with Lucinda.

The station in Kentucky not only had pilots, but also Medical Administrators, Medical Officers and Air Evacuation nurses. After a day or two it was obvious we were there awaiting further orders. Our only requirement was to call in each morning and learn whether orders for the next station had been received. Lucinda had left me off at the base one morning and found an apartment near the base and a large city park. I remember that it had a large kitchen and how Lucinda moved around to prepare our breakfast and evening meals. We rented bicycles, and, after calling the base and finding no orders, we cycled to Cherokee Park and had a picnic lunch. This went on for most of September. The weather was wonderful, and we were quite fit and much in love. One day we called and learned that we had orders to go to San Antonio and the School of Aviation Medicine.

It was early October 1942 when we left Kentucky. Before I describe our trip to Texas, I must mention that I had learned that my mentor, Ludwig Eichna, MD, had become a commissioned officer and was stationed at the Armed Forces Research Center at Fort Knox. We arranged to meet him, and had a long weekend when the three of us made a trip south and east (to my old Kentucky home), then north to Lexington and along the Ohio back to Fort Knox and Louisville. Ike was great. Clearly, he was bachelor oriented, and Lucinda liked him very much. I told him of my orders to Texas by phone and he wished me luck. I did not see or hear from him again until April 1946, when we met at the Research Society meetings in Atlantic City. Lucinda drove and I was the navigator. Little do I remember of our trip. We passed through Little Rock, Arkansas. I noted the downtown area, a large hotel, the Abner McGehee. Later

I learned that our 4th year Chief Resident, and after World War II, Osler Professor of Medicine at Hopkins, A.M. Harvey, was named after the same person as the hotel. Few of his contemporaries knew what the initials A.M. stood for.

Our arrival in San Antonio was on one of the most beautiful days; warm and sunny that I recall. We reported to the school, (SAM), and learned I was assigned to the Aviation Physiology course. That was what I had hoped! Classes were to begin on the next Monday. Lucinda looked and looked for a place to stay, as we were told we would be there for 2 to 3 months. We found a furnished house in Alamo Heights, not far from Randolph, and we signed up for a three month contract.

Lucinda would drive me to the base in the morning so she would have the car and could explore the area. In the late afternoon, she either picked me up or I arranged for a fellow student to drop me off in Alamo Heights. Usually he and I would have a drink with Lucinda for the service. The only fellow officer I recall was Francis Chinard, Hopkins '41, who was in the same class at Randolph. We three partied together. I had told Ward Fowler, MD S '37 about this program, and he was either in the class ahead or the class following. Later I learned that both Fowler and Chinard were assigned to the Altitude Training Program in England. They were instructors in the heavy bombing groups of the 8th Air Force.

At the same time we were at SAM, there was a class of MDs being trained as Flight Surgeons. They were usually General Duty Officers, but some were Ophthalmologists or ENT Specialists. Those in our group were MDs and Physiology PhDs many of whom were Pulmonary Physiologists. As I look back on our course of instruction, we learned most of what we needed to know in the first six weeks. Then there was two to four weeks when we were involved in "hands on" operation of the low pressure chamber to indoctrinate the primary school pilots and the flight surgeon, as to when oxygen was to be used at the higher altitudes (i.e. low pressure). Then there was another period of waiting for orders.

I don't recall why Lucinda had to walk to New Braunfels that Thanksgiving to get our turkey, but she did, and Chinard and another classmate whose name I don't recall, shared it with us in our beautiful house in Alamo Heights.

It was just before Christmas 1942 that I received orders for my first duty station. It was to be at Pyote Air Base, Second Air Force in West Texas, near Monahans and Wink and 50 miles east of the Pecos River on the main E-W Highway to El Paso. I was to be the director of the 1311 High Altitude Training Center at Pyote Air Base. This base was built to accommodate B-17 bombers with ten to twelve man crews. When we arrived in this part of West Texas, we found that the base was a distance of 10 to 15 miles from the nearest community. We were able to rent a one floor house in the town of Monahans, 15 miles east of the base. The Pecos town and river were 50 miles west. On both sides of the runway were buildings, many under construction. My recall is that there was a base headquarters, an operations center, a half dozen barracks, a mess hall and the base hospital.

I was to direct the 1311th Altitude Training Unit (ATU), which was under construction. This was adjacent to and connected by a corridor to the north wing of the hospital. The Base Surgeon was my commanding officer. His name was Ten Hooten and the Base Commander was Colonel Hewitt. The low pressure chamber, a steel cylinder, was on a freight car on a railroad siding on the base; a "spur" of tracks to the base had been built on a siding from the railroad running west to El Paso from Abilene. Pyote was essentially a crossroads running north and south over the highway to El Paso. Five miles northeast was Wink, an oil field with flames burning 24/7. There were no B-17s on the base, but they were expected any day with crews returning from service in the Pacific. There they were stationed in Townsville, Australia, and had completed their tour, bombing Jap bases in New Guinea. This kept the Japanese out of Northern Australia.

My recollection is that Captain Ten Houten (a Dutch descendant from Michigan) did not know anything about the Altitude Training Program. He authorized me to go to the office of the Base Commander. Colonel Hewitt talked to me briefly and had one of his associates get out the base plan and drawings, and from this I was shown a table of organization (TO). This described the mission, the number of officers (MD and PhD) and Medical Administrators (1) and enlisted men (15). The Altitude Training was part of a detailed training of air crews, whose basic training as pilots, navigators, radio operators, etc. had taken place at other bases. Gunnery training was part of the Pyote mission.

The Cadre of New Guinea veterans was to give "real warfare experience" to supplement and/or complement the basic training. The HQ personnel section early had no information about when the men ordered to 1311th ATU would be arriving. In the meantime, I interacted with the other MDs of the base hospital and I believe I also served as Medical Officer of the day. The chief activity on the base for the MDs (there were a few patients in the hospital because of injuries in ground accidents), was a volleyball game in the middle of the day in January and February. It would be freezing at night but from 60-70 from 11-3 each day, sun shining daily. During this period, the ATU building received the low pressure chamber and personnel began to arrive. This was in February. We learned to operate it by taking turns (officers and enlisted men) as subjects, and by mid to late March we were inviting Captains to come over with their crews and tell us how they used their oxygen equipment in New Guinea, and how we might incorporate their experience in our program. I should state that sometime in the January-February period over 3-4 days, 5 planes arrived, then 10 the next day and 10 more the day after, all with their crews.

The Second Air Force had bases in many Western states. The weather interference in the Northwest with the training and emergency situations led to the order to Colonel Hewitt to prepare for an entire operational B-17 training group to be transferred from the Boise, Idaho base in the next two to three days. The ATU had to increase the number of Airmen trained, in order to accommodate the need for more trained crews to be sent to England, North Africa and the South Pacific. The Air Surgeon's office was being contacted frequently because of problems in function, but we had no reason to contact Washington. This we learned when I received orders to report to the Aero Medical Laboratory in Wright Field, Dayton, Ohio in late April.

Lucinda and I were getting accustomed to West Texas life and interacting with the other couples, and on weekends exploring towns in the vicinity and meeting many friends of a Stackhouse widow, Aunt Grace. She lived in El Paso in the winter, and was on her ranch in San Antonio, New Mexico the rest of the year.

Cuernavaca 1943

In January, we were able to get a week's leave, and drove into Nuevo Laredo Mexico to visit Monterey and Mexico City. Lucinda had a miscarriage and was in touch with her Obstetrician in Philadelphia who reassured her that this was not unusual. She also had an invitation from her Chief of X-Ray at Penn as to whether she would consider a job at HUP as the coordinator of the HUP Tumor Clinic, should I be sent overseas. This was the background of our situation as my orders arrived for the ATU conference in Dayton.

Orders were issued in late April 1943 for detached service: "Conference of ATU Directors." Using the Commercial Air, I flew back to Ohio and reported to HQ Material Command, US Army Air Corps, Wright Field. I was assigned to a barracks and was told where to report at 0800 the next morning. The remainder of the day I met others in ATU services and they were mostly PhDs in Physiology. All were on duty in training bases in the USA. Most of our conversations related to what were the individual's background and interests before going on active duty.

The meeting was called to order by a Medical Officer, now a Colonel, who was one of the principal instructors at Randolph Field for the Aviation Physiologists. My recollection is that he was one of the few MD Physiologists whose career was teaching and administration in a Medical School Department of Physiology. Other leaders of the program were introduced, and Professor Detlev Bronk of the University of Pennsylvania was there, and he spoke briefly, a message of welcome. A program was announced and the format was an introduction by a leader of the conference.

Then this was followed by questions and answers to problems cited by ATU directors. A given subject was discussed for an hour, and then there was a coffee break and informal discussion for 30 minutes, then back to the conference room. My guess is that there were about 20 ATU directors in attendance.

Another two aspects of the ATU operation were discussed, and again "feedback" from the ATU directors. Soon it was 12:30 and we adjourned for lunch. The organizers sat at different tables and informal discussion continued. Then there was an afternoon session less organized, and many directors were asked to take the floor and make a statement about how they were attempting to do their job and what cooperation they were getting from their Base HQ. It was quite informal, and I don't recall how it was that I had the opportunity of talking to Detlev Bronk alone for ten to fifteen minutes. At that time I told him that I was content with my job, but that my wife and I had discussed whether I might seek an overseas assignment; and she, having the offer of the Tumor Clinic job at HUP, was willing for me to try to get an overseas assignment.

I asked Dr. Bronk if he thought that might be possible. I was surprised when he said he remembered seeing a request to the Air Surgeon from a Regular Army Flight Surgeon heading the Medical Department for the crews "flying the Hump" from bases in Assam, India having made such a request not too long ago. Bronk said he had not received a response from the Air Surgeon's Office in Washington. He asked, "Are you willing to serve in India?" Without hesitation, I said, "Yes." The reply was, "If the individual has not yet been assigned, do you want me to recommend you?" Again, I said yes. We shook hands and I thanked him for his advice and help. Bronk did this, and it was not too long afterwards that I heard that a replacement was to be sent to Pyote and that in "due time" I would be sent "leave orders" in preparation for an overseas assignment.

In the meantime I continued my daily routine at Pyote, having told only Lucinda, my wife, about what happened. It was in late June, when I received "leave orders" and Lucinda and I drove back to Youngstown and visited my parents at 360 Fairgreen.

My mother convinced Lucinda that she should have a new Ford Coupe, which somehow my mother knew she could get from a dealer friend in Youngstown. Lucinda hated to give up her '34 convertible, which had a relatively new canvas top that we were able to get the previous September in Louisville. But she went along with the plan and we drove back to Philadelphia in a new black '41 and '42 model 4 passenger coupe, that had gone 5 miles.

Our first objective was to get an apartment for Lucinda, as we were staying temporarily with the Pennypackers at 6676 MacCallum. This was a piece of good luck, that in a few days, there was an available, vacant, newly refinished apartment-411 The Kenilworth in Alden Park, Germantown. We moved some of Lucinda's possessions from Uncle Aubrey's attic and Mary Ferguson offered some of hers, so that in a short time the 411 was furnished and we moved in.

Youngstown April 1942

Next, Lucinda contacted the HUP X-Ray Department and Dr. Prendergrass was pleased to hear that she was back in Philadelphia and ready to work. By this time, we had an address and a phone number and I contacted the Pyote Base HQ and told them where to send my orders. I was told by the Adjutant that as of late August nothing had been received.

Within a week or so I was called and told that I was to report, after Labor Day, to the Adjutant in Morrison Field Air Base, West Palm Beach, and await overseas orders at the Air Transport Command Base there, HQ Caribbean Wing.

On arrival at the Florida-Air Transport Command, Morrison Field in West Palm Beach, I discovered that this was a pool of enlisted men and officers stationed in "transit" barracks. They were all awaiting orders for as long as four weeks, more at least two weeks, and many, many men who had been there at least one week. The process was to contact the Adjutant at 0800 each day, and if no orders, one was free to do whatever one wished for the next 24 hours, then repeat the process. I learned that the big famous hotel, The Breakers, on the Atlantic at Palm Beach, was now a General Hospital, and that the recreation duty officer was friendly and allowed officers to use the beach. I rode over there on a rented bicycle and introduced myself as a Medical Officer on temporary duty at Morrison Field. I gave him my name and he gave me a phone extension number. He welcomed me, showed me the changing room for men, and said I could use the beach any time I wanted during the life guard on duty hours. I asked if I might give the Morrison Field his extension number.

I also rode around looking for apartment units for rent in West

West Palm Beach 1943

Palm Beach. After several days, still in the first seven days after arrival, I found an apartment which I could rent on a monthly basis for an amount that we could afford. It was located in the most eastern part of West Palm Beach, i.e. near to the causeway for a bicycle ride to the Breakers General Hospital. That evening I called Lucinda and asked if she was a "gambler." The gamble was that, if she now came to Florida, we might have a "Palm Beach Honeymoon" for a day, a week, or if lucky, a month, all on "Uncle Sam." She said she would have to check with the HUP physicians (who were not yet organized, as the medical students were not yet back for the new academic year), and get their reaction to her suggestions that she would like to delay her full time attendance for another two to three weeks. They gave her the OK and she was able to get a train booking in the next few days. So I moved from the barracks into the apartment complex and made a deal with the bicycle rental group to be on a weekly rental fee, rather than a more expensive daily fee.

Within a week of my call, Lucinda was with me at the ELCID apartments in West Palm Beach. The weather was like mid-summer, and we explored the area on our rented bicycles. We saw some fresh cherries on a stand, and Lucinda, knowing my favorite pie, baked several in the ELCID kitchen.

The most memorable experience was started by a notice on the Breakers General Hospital bulletin board (we went to that beach after breakfast each morning and stayed the duration of life guard duty hours), that a British American Palm Beach resident, who had lived in China and Burma, was to give a lecture on "The Burma Road." We attended the lecture, which was fascinating, and after the lecture, we introduced ourselves to the speaker. He was told about my assignment to the India China Wing, ATC. He was most enthusiastic about living in that part of the world, asked for our phone number and said he would be in touch. Not too long afterwards, a day or so, he invited us to join him and his wife at a dinner party at their home in Palm Beach a day or so in the future. We did, and we had a wonderful time. He told us about his Jade collection which he was arranging to give to the Norton Public Art Gallery in West Palm Beach. He had compiled a picture book of his collection and gave Lucinda an autographed copy. That was the highlight of our Palm Beach honeymoon.

Lucinda and I were there for another two weeks when my orders came in to move to Miami Beach. Lucinda decided to go there with me. We stayed at another "transit" barracks, this time a large Miami Beach hotel. I was there perhaps three or four days when orders came to be ready to fly out of Miami Beach at 24 hours notice. Then I arranged for Lucinda to fly back to Philadelphia. In a few days, I was on an ATC plane, with our first stop in Puerto Rico, and destination Brazil.

After an overnight stop in Guyana, at that time still a British Colony, we flew another full day in an ATC DC3 plane and landed in Eastern Brazil on the coast north of Recife. That is where we were at least a week, perhaps more. We were in a "transit" barracks, and if one had no orders at 0800 Roll Call, the times of the trucks leaving for the beach some five miles away were announced. The beach was shallow. One walked out at least 200 yards before the water was waist deep. There air filled wet cotton mattress covers were used to float us in. Fresh pineapple was our lunch at a penny per pineapple. After 10 days or so, orders came to cross the South Atlantic.

Ascencion is a small island with few inhabitants. It was a naval station and part of the British St. Helena Colony. ATC had constructed an airbase on what seemed like black volcanic rock. Our plane was a DC3. We were there long enough only to refuel. We took off and headed for the ATC Base at Accra. That was on the coast of West Africa, where the coastline runs west to east. Then Accra was the Capital of the Gold Coast, with about 150 thousand inhabitants. The passengers on this transatlantic flight were put in the charge of an ATC officer who assigned us to "transit" barracks and briefed us as to how we would receive further travel orders as planes became available. I learned that a fellow staff member of the Hospital of the University of Pennsylvania, Curtis Dohan, was assigned there as a General Duty Medical Officer.

Before my orders to go had arrived, I spent time with him to learn what he was doing, and later, while at Penn, we would recall those days. The route I traveled I learned had been built by Pan American Officials in the late 30s. We made frequent stops in the DC3 as we traversed Middle Africa ending up in Khartoum as an overnight stop. Then it was south along the Nile to Aden on the South Coast of the Arabian Peninsula where, (although it was a free port), the air base was part of the British Empire. This was an important ATC Base. We stayed overnight there and soon an ATC plane moved us to the "transit" barracks of ATC at Karachi on the West Coast of India. Many officers and enlisted men were there awaiting their orders to go to other parts of India and many to China. It was early in October that I arrived in the large ATC Hub in Assam at Chabua, in India's most eastern province. The airbases were built in tea gardens around Chabua, as part of the US-British "lend lease."

Chabua 1943

After arrival there and assignment to the transit barracks, I received orders to report to Major Smith, Chief Medical Officer of the ATC Base. Dr. Smith was an ENT Specialist from Little Rock, and he told me that I was to be part of his medical detachment temporarily. This was because the Hump Flying Training School Project was not yet operative. He asked me what I would like to do in the interval, and I said I would like to work with him as a Medical Officer General Duty. Soon he told me I was to serve as a Medical Officer at a new hump flying base starting up in the lower Brahmaputra Valley west of Jorhat. This was Mismari.

There I worked with Medical Officers, specifically, Charles Kirby, who later came to U of PA as a surgeon on the Ravdin Staff. Our Medical CO was Major Waldorf. I was not stationed there more than 6 to 8 weeks, and I was ordered back to Chabua to again be part of Major Smith's staff. A new Officer's area was being opened up, in the middle of a tea garden, for flying officers going from Chabua on China flights. Major Smith had arranged for me to have a "Basha" in the new area and work with his Clinical Staff in the Dispensary, near the runway, for sick calls.

While I was doing this, I met many officers going on to China, saw General Chenault and Admiral Mountbatten, and met some officers from the Penn 20th General Hospital in Ledo, Assam, who were going back on ATC to the USA. One was Major Sergeant Pepper, MD, a son of the late Dean, my friend, William Pepper, MD.

While there in Chabua, I was told to meet with the ATC Deputy Chief, Colonel Ed Abbey, who was about to assign me to go with a group to rescue "down air crews," somewhere in Southern Tibet. I asked permission to discuss this assignment with General Don Flickinger, whom I had met only briefly, earlier, soon after arriving in Chabua. General Flickinger was very cordial, and decided, personally, to learn what he could about the "down air crew mission." I was with him, and he found it was all very vague. He said to me," You go back to what you were doing. Soon our Hump-flying School will begin operating and you will be assigned there."

The ATC base at Gaya was selected because the all year around flying conditions were better in this area nearer to Agra and

Calcutta, with minor monsoon weather. The base was to be commanded by Colonel Joseph Mountrin, ICW, ATC. Mountrin was a veteran airline pilot and was known to be, because of his personality and tact, one of the best commanders in the India China Wing. I was to be the Aviation Physiologist and interact with the other school faculty, (pilots who had flown across the mountains into China fifty times or more, but had not yet been 12 months in the India China Wing), in classes.

Our job was to update the new pilots on how to get across, unload their cargo, and return to Assam with their plane intact and ready for another trip. The planes would fly at an altitude of 15,000 feet or more for most of the flight. I also learned that the Medical Officer at Gaya was being returned to the USA and I was to be Head of the Medical Detachment and Chief Medical Officer of the base. Within two or three months the project was coordinated so that new flying officers coming to ICW ATC, were assigned to Gaya. They lived on the base, and were instructed in classes and had solo flying assignments

Darjeeling 1944

with veteran copilots. Within a two to three week period, they were evaluated and, if competent, were assigned to one of the many hump flying bases in Assam. The school was running smoothly and Colonel Mountrin was recalled to the US. He was followed by a less competent C.O., Colonel Willey who was given the responsibility of enlarging the base so that there was another living area. Another Medical Officer and a Dental Officer was also assigned and they were housed in the new area some two to three miles from the runways. By January 1945 more and more supplies were being moved into China each month. B-29 planes were also in the area and were making several flights each day over the Hump to carry more plane fuel into Western China. Soon, B-29s were making raids from Western China on the Japanese home islands, although the coast area of China was occupied by both Japanese Air and Ground Units.

In April or May 1945 I was told by Gaya Base HQ that the base was to be visited by a representative of the Air Surgeon's Office. I was to be the host of the visiting officer and was surprised when this turned out to be Major David Bishop-Swarthmore '35-a PhD in Biology and a protégé of Professor Detlev Bronk, Swarthmore '21. His orders obviously had originated from the office of the Air Surgeon. But why? He told me that he would like to see what my responsibilities, i.e. duties, were over several 24 hour periods. We met at breakfast and he would shadow me all morning and afternoon (after our 1-2PM siesta). He stayed several days before he had to go on to Calcutta. Time passed quickly and my fellow roommates-Joe Halsmer, Chief Flying Officer, and Jack Beaver, Deputy Base Commander, told me they were planning a "leave" in early June in the mountains near Simla, the summer government capital. They invited me to join them, and I made arrangements with the C.O. and my associate-Dr. Joseph Lowenthal, an alumnus of Penn Medical School. It was in early June, 1945 when we arrived in Simla and learned that the Viceroy of India had called a conference of Hindus and Muslims to discuss how, after the British left, they would govern India in the post war period. The accommodations were all in use and the first night we slept on make-shift cots on the stage of the dance hall in the largest hotel for Europeans-The Lord Cecil. With bribes to the Swiss Manager,(cigarettes and liquor), we did better later.

At one point the three of us gave a bachelor beer party to honor the Australian High Commission to India, Lt. General Ivan Mackay, a veteran of the New Guinea and North African Campaigns. He was very pleased and introduced us to his wife and daughter. Soon we were invited to all sorts of receptions. Our ten day "leave" flew by and a plane was sent from our base in Gaya to pick us up at the Royal Air Force Base near Simla, and so ended an unexpected "hegira."

I was just getting back into the usual routine at Gaya in early July 1945, when the Deputy Commander, Jack A. Beaver, told me that orders had been received to return me to the United States for duty at the Aero Medical Laboratory at Wright Field, Dayton, Ohio no later than 1 August. By the time I arrived in Karachi, one Atomic bomb had been dropped by a B-29. My orders seemed to get me a priority return straight back, as I remember being in the Persian Gulf near Abadam, at midnight, when the temperature was 110 degrees F. The plane refueled and we immediately flew west. Soon I was in a "transit camp" outside of Cairo with many other officers, most of whom seemed to be heading from the Middle East and Southern Europe bases to the USA for the Japan mission. Many of the flights back were in a DC3 with very young pilots. By the time I arrived in Casablanca, Japan had surrendered and they were celebrating V-J Day.

Soon I was on a plane from Casablanca to the Azores, Bermuda, and then Miami. I was put with a group of officers and enlisted men on a train from Miami and I ended up in a camp in Greensboro, North Carolina. There I was given orders to go by train to Indiantown Gap, Pa, for leave orders with instructions that my next duty station, after a thirty day leave, was to be the Aero Medical Laboratory in Dayton, Ohio on September 15.

Autumn 1945

I had last seen Lucinda in Miami Beach in late September 1943 when I had received my orders to fly to India. Returning to the USA by air from Bermuda to Miami in early August 1945, I went, by train, to Greensboro, N.C. After a day or so there, I received orders to go, by train, to the Pennsylvania Military Base, Indiantown Gap. While on this train, I learned that the train would stop at the Pennsylvania Station in Washington, but not in Philadelphia, before going west to the Gap. Lucinda knew I was on the way to Indiantown Gap. When I decided to leave the troop train in Washington, I called her to tell her the arrival time of the train I would be taking from Washington to the 30th Street Station. She said she would meet me there and would drive me to the Gap Base early the next morning. This plan worked, and by 11 A.M. the next day, I was on leave and we were driving back to 411 Kenilworth in Alden Park, Germantown, free until 15 September. On the trip back to 411, Lucinda told me that her younger brother, Powell, who had served two years with the Quartermaster Corps at Abadan on the Persian Gulf, would be back in the USA sometime in the next week. Lucinda and Barbara, Powell's wife, (whom I had never met), had arranged that we would go to Northeast Harbor, Maine, and stay at the hotel known as the Kimball House the last half of August. I unpacked in 411 and soon Powell was home. We then met in town at a men's store, Jacob Reeds, where we were measured for new dress slacks and jackets to go along with our best khakis. This was needed because at that time the only clothes we had were what we were wearing. We both had lost from 30 pounds in the two years in the hot climate.

After the clothes were fitted, we were off to Maine, making the trip in one day. Powell and Barbara were in her car, and I was in Lucinda's Ford Coupe. Our plan was to go west from Maine to Youngstown to visit with my parents. Then I was going to go from there to Dayton for duty on 15 September. Barbara and Powell returned to Philadelphia and looked for a house. They found a small farm on Shiloh Road near Westtown and West Chester.

The vacation was wonderful. For the last two weeks of August, it rained almost every day. But that did not stop us from sailing, playing golf, and exploring Acadia National Park. One sunny day we played tennis with borrowed tennis shoes, racquets, and balls. Since it was cold, many guests had left just after V-J Day, and the four of us were the only ones in the Kimball House dining room for breakfast and dinner for the last ten days of our stay. The Innkeeper, Loren Kimball, hovered over us at each meal, insisting that Powell and I have second helpings. Thus, in two weeks we gained back what we had lost in two years and another fitting at Jacob Reed's was necessary by the time we returned to Philadelphia.

For our vacation Uncle Aubrey had recommended 'old style' summer hotels in New Hampshire and Vermont. We stayed two nights in each place, peopled with affluent, much older, guests. I was the only one in uniform, and Lucinda, an Arthur Murray dancing instructor for four years after she graduated from Swarthmore, and I were often the only ones on the dance floor, with the orchestra playing songs from South Pacific. Our trip through Vermont, New York State and into Ohio was uneventful. We visited my parents for about a week before I went by train to Dayton. Lucinda drove her car back to 411.

When I reported to Dr. Gagge at Wright Field in the autumn of 1945 I was informed that, after the surrender of Japan, there was a need for preparation of summaries of the experience of Air Force Officers in the many theatres of operation. Dr. Gagge was a PhD Physiologist who was on the Yale Medical School Faculty who I assumed was also a Detlev Bronk recruit. He told me that now that the wars were over, it was a time for closing down, and summarizing the war experience. We talked in a general way about the experience I had as an Aviation Physiologist and Gaya Base Chief Medical Officer. When I told him that one of my fellow officers, a Psychiatrist, Dr. Henry Wegrocki, (who was rotated out of the CBI Theatre earlier than I), had given me a copy of a report he wrote about Psychological and Psychiatric problems of Hump fliers, he said he wanted me to write down what I told him about my experience and to integrate Dr. Wegrocki's experiences in this report. This is what I set out to do. While at the Aero-Medical, I learned that I was returned because Major Bishop had reported that his investigation showed that what I was doing at Gaya might be done by a Medical Officer, General Duty. My classification as an Aviation Physiologist and service with the Hump Flying Officers of ICW ATC was thought to be more useful in the Aero Medical Laboratory Projects that were then, in early summer 1945, undermanned.

While there, Colonel Gagge, gave me several leaves, i.e. "long weekends." I went back to Lucinda each time. On one of these,

Lucinda and I drove around the Northern and Western suburbs of Philadelphia and looked at houses that were planned and being The area that seemed the most suitable was in Penn-Wynne in the Haverford-Manoa Road area, across City Line from West Philadelphia.

I was not there long when Dr. Gagge introduced me to an Air Force Physiology Consultant, Professor Carl Schmidt of the University of Pennsylvania School of Medicine. Schmidt was there as a guest and gave a brief lecture on what research was going on in his Pharmacology Department Laboratory on brain blood flow and the neural controls of respiration. It was my good fortune to be awarded a Rockefeller Foundation Fellowship for Veterans by Dr. Schmidt. He said I could start on 15 December at a salary of $1800 per year, this being the start of 2nd year medical students teaching period. I quickly finished the report and informed Colonel Gagge that I had accepted Dr. Schmidt's Rockefeller Foundation Fellowship to teach and do research in Pharmacology at U of PA. The date teaching of second year medical students in that department was scheduled to begin on 15 December, 1945. Dr. Gagge asked me if I wanted to be there at the beginning. I said yes. He then helped me to summarize and conclude my project. On another leave before 15 December, I arranged to see Dr. O. H. Perry Pepper. I told him I wanted to come back to the Department of Medicine after I had updated my knowledge of Physiology and Pharmacology, and have resident, i.e. house officer training under his leadership. He accepted me and urged me to keep him informed of my progress and future plans, now that he was aware I had married Lucinda in July 1942, and that we were expecting.

Dr. Gagge's staff found that I had accumulated leave that extended into February 1946. He also recommended me for a terminal promotion to Major, M. C., on my discharge, and thus I left the Aero Medical to be in Philadelphia for the start of the teaching semester in December. In early 1946, Dr. Gagge wrote me and thanked me for my efforts. He returned the typed report to me which I carried around for years. One day I came across it and decided it should be discarded.

6. Life With Lucinda T. Hafkenschiel: 1946-83

We signed up for a house to be built at 1458 Hampstead Road in Penn Wynne. This house was to cost $10,750. Mr. Holden, the builder/contractor, said that for $2500 more he would finish the second floor, providing a full bathroom, two bedrooms and a large storage room. We agreed after discussing it with Uncle Aubrey and moved in 30 May, 1946. This location was a better commute to the University of Pennsylvania, than that from Germantown. I was introduced to Drs. Schmidt, Conroe, Katy and Bruner. They were longtime members of the department and were most helpful to newcomers such as Jim Eckenhof, J.K. Clark and Charles Landmesser. Lucinda had completed her duties as an Administrator for the HUP Tumor Clinic and was doing well with the pregnancy, along with plans and purchases for furnishing the house at 1458.

Penn Wynne House

The teaching of second year students in Pharmacology was fascinating, and Dr. Schmidt was suggesting different research projects, seeing that I was more interested in Cardiovascular Physiology and Pharmacology than anything else. I was using a frog heart perfusion model and testing the effects of various sodium and potassium solutions on the heart pumping action. This was not too encouraging, and I welcomed Dr. Schmidt's suggestion that another WWII Veteran in the Department, James Eckenhoff, MD, needed help in a project he had started. This involved measuring blood flow to the heart in anesthetized dogs using a bubble flow meter. Jim was planning to go into Anesthesiology training after a year in Pharmacology. His project worked out well, leading eventually to several research publications. We postponed our move to Clinical Departments, staying on in Pharmacology from 1945 to 1948. Then we both moved to the Hospital of the University of Pennsylvania with Jim as Resident in Anesthesiology and I in

Medicine. The Pharmacology Department had several experienced teachers. These were Julius Comroe, David Brunner and Seymour Kety. Younger recruits were Landmesser, Harmel, Foltz, Clark and Lambertson; all of whom participated in the teaching which was completed for the academic year 1945-1946 on 31 March, 1946. Dr. Julius Comroe lived in the Penn Wynne area, and he offered to drive me into Penn with him each weekday. I did this after we moved into 1458 in late May. Julius was one of my best mentors.

Dr. F. Sidney Dunne was Lucinda's Obstetrician. I had met him and liked him. He planned to admit Lucinda to his Obstetric service at the Pennsylvania Hospital where he was associated with Dr. Kimbrough at 8th and Spruce. Lucinda began to have labor pains early on 6 June, and I drove her to the Pennsylvania Hospital where she was admitted. The pains quieted, so I went out to Penn for a research meeting. The pains returned, however, and she soon delivered our first son which I learned about over the phone.

Our work in Pharmacology, in 1946-7, centered on the transfer of coronary blood flow in dogs studied using the bubble flow meter for the nitrous oxide measurement of coronary blood flow. This required the use of a venous catheter introduced from the jugular vein into the coronary sinus- i.e. the major vein draining the heart muscle. Kety had introduced this method of measuring brain blood flow by having a large needle into the jugular vein of humans to measure the level of inhaled nitrous oxide for a fifteen minute period draining brain venous blood into the jugular. Arterial levels were obtained by blood drawn from major arteries. These studies were productive and publications were planned comparing both methods as studied in Penn's Pharmacology Department. These studies lead to publications which are enumerated in a collected reprint book which I have given to my son, Tom. In 1947, my salary was increased from $1800 to $2000 a year.

Kety was in Atlantic City in the spring research meeting period of April-May 1948 when he was independently approached by two investigators, Walter Goodale and Richard Bing, on the same day. He was asked if a catheter could be introduced into the coronary sinus of a dog, a primate, or a human, might the nitrous oxide method of measuring brain blood flow be adapted to measuring coronary artery blood flow? Kety said yes. Such a study was underway in dogs in the Pharmacology Department at Penn, undertaken by Eckenhoff and JHH Jr. This led to a meeting several months later at Penn with Professor Schmidt, Eckenhoff, Walter Goodale and Richard Bing. By this time, Comroe and Kety had left the Pharmacology Department and were colleagues in the Department of Physiology and Pharmacology in the Graduate School of the University of PA.

This collaboration required that Goodale would work with Bing in patients at Hopkins on the technique of introducing a catheter in the coronary sinus of conscious patients. Eckenhoff and I traveled to Hopkins several times on day trips and were present when Bing and colleagues used the nitrous oxide method. A publication in the American Heart Journal in 1950 was the result of what was then a historic collaboration. Eckenhoff and I went into the Clinical Departments as of 1 July 1947.

The summer of 1947 was the second summer that I served as a junior "attending" on the medical wards of the Hospital of the University of PA. I had heard about Baruch Fellowship in "Medical Instrumentation" in the Graduate School at M.I.T. Although these were conceived as a scientific background for physicians planning a career in Rehabilitation Medicine, I sent a request for detailed information and an application form.

My plan, under Dr. Pepper, was to start as a Resident in September 1947. When he learned that from my inquiry that I would be accepted in the program at MIT beginning 1 Sept. '47, he agreed to pay my salary for that semester, and urged me to attend. Lucinda was expecting and was too involved with the care of JHH III to be too concerned about what I was doing to further my career as a Clinical Pharmacologist with a particular interest in cardiovascular applications. Sometime in this period when I was doing ward work in medicine in the summer months, I learned from Dr. George Gammon, the Professor of Neurology, that a Swiss Pharmaceutical Company representative had told him about an ergot derived drug, that they were hoping would improve brain blood flow in post-stroke patients. I told him I was interested but did not know what I could do about it until I returned from the fall semester study in the Graduate School MIT Biology Department. I needed to know more about this newer technology.

It was at this point that on 1 August 1947, early in the morning, Lucinda went into labor. I drove her to HUP and found Dr. George Hoffman awaiting her arrival, as Dr. Dunne was on vacation. Within an hour or so, Tom was delivered. Lucinda was well and happy, and Tom was named after her father.

As planned, I went to MIT where I was given a room in the Graduate House with roommate Dr. Jesse Scott. I commuted back and forth, returning on Friday evening and going back to Cambridge on Sunday evenings. I worked in Student Health to earn extra money. When I was at 1458, Lucinda asked me to care for Tom as he cried all the time during my absence. I found out that a full bottle satisfied him and so kept him quiet while I spent 48-72 hours each weekend at 1458. The winter was rigorous, but soon it was February and I returned to Lucinda, Joe and Tom. Then I began my duty as the Resident in Medicine responsible for ward admissions. This I did until 1 July 1948.

During the period when I was Assistant Resident for Ward Admissions, I explored possibilities of how I might learn Clinical Cardiology by working in that specialty clinic. After discussions with Dr. Charles Wolferth, who was Chief of the Cardiovascular section with Dr. Kay, Cardiology, Dr. Jeffers, Hypertension and Dr. Montgomery, Peripheral Vascular Disease, Dr. Wolferth decided I should be with Dr. Jeffers in the Hypertension section. Dr. Wolferth's wife had

With Tom at Penn Wynne

been in trouble with severe hypertension and she was not helped by a sympathectomy. He was planning to add adrenalectomy to the surgical approach and was optimistic that there was a future for drug therapy of essential hypertension and that my Pharmacology Department experience might be an asset in that section.

In a short time after beginning my Cardiology Fellowship, 1 July 1948 to 1949, I was being contacted by drug makers asking for clinical trials of potentially useful antihypertensive agents. First, there was Squibb, with Rauwolfia Products, then Ciba with Serpasil and Apresoline, Wyeth with hexamethonium, and Sandoz with dihydroergocornine. Diuretics were on the horizon. It was soon evident that the drugs were helpful to patients with moderate hypertension, but of little value in patients with severe diastolic hypertension and early kidney function impairment. Two studies were undertaken: 1) for severe hypertension sympathectomy with bilateral adrenalectomy, and 2) antihypertensive drugs for those rejecting surgery or having only moderate hypertension.

In this period up to 1 July 1949, I was working in the Hypertension Clinic two days a week, serving as a consultant in drug treatment of hypertensive patients on the medical wards, and writing grant proposals to obtain funds to set up a laboratory in which our group might work. Our plan was to measure cerebral blood flow before and after the blood pressure was lowered by a parenteral dose of an antihypertensive agent. Our good luck was the timing as well as the opportunity to getting space in HUP. The 9th floor Gates Building in 1950 was ready for occupancy and, just before he retired, Dr. Wolferth saw to it that the space was made available for our own studies. Our group had moved up to 9th Gates from third Maloney. Dr. F.C. Wood had become chairman of the Medicine Department and chief of the cardiovascular section. Dr. Wolferth moved his private office from HUP to 36th and Walnut. He had private patients in beds in the HUP and I would make rounds with him every morning from 0730 to at least 0930. Having the academic rank of Instructor in Medicine and Clinical Pharmacology and private practice privileges in offices on the third floor of the Maloney Building before moving to 9th Gates, I started a private practice, having most of my patients referred either by Dr. Wolferth or by his cadre of outside referring practitioners.

My grant requests to the National Heart Institute were approved. I hired and trained technicians using the Kety nitrous oxide blood flow method and was able to get several young MDs to be part of my team. These were Crumpton, Harmel, and Moyer. The first drug we tested in humans was Dihydroergocornine. Our study was the first to show that when the blood pressure was lowered by administering this drug, brain blood flow remained unchanged and within normal limits. This was my first report in the Journal of Clinical Investigation, considered to be one of the more prestigious journals at that time.

Lucinda and I had arranged to have a vacation for two weeks in a rented house at Brant Beach, Long Beach Island, in July 1948 and again in July 1949. Joe and Tom flourished there as did Lucinda who was a good swimmer. A happy event came when Mark Conroy Hafkenschiel, named for my maternal grandfather, was born in the Hospital of the University of Pennsylvania on February 8, 1950 . Later that year, I was elected to Sigma XI at Penn, and was inducted as a fellow into the College of Physicians of Philadelphia. On July 1 1951, I was given the academic rank of Associate in Medicine in the Department of Medicine and was a staff member of the Department of Medicine of HUP. My first assignment as Senior Attending was on the Pepper Ward at the time Mark arrived in early 1950.

It was in this period that Lucinda was teaching first day school at the Merion Friends Meeting and Joe and Tom were in pre-school classes there. The Chief was Mrs. Spiller, whose brother was a prominent pediatrician and whose husband was a Professor at Penn. The commute from Penn Wynne was difficult and Lucinda had contacted several agents as to housing closer to the Merion Friends Meeting but no decision was made to move. We again visited Long Beach Island in the summers of 1950 and 1951.

I volunteered to do some Philadelphia area fundraising for M.I.T. and was assigned to a team headed by Brydon (Bud) Greene. We visited prospects at their homes in the evening. One such prospect was the father of an MIT graduate who lived on Heath Road in Merion, two houses off Bowman Avenue. This prospect was Walter Karcher, then

Young Family at Penn Wynne

in his 70s. He was a prominent Philadelphian architect, and I had first learned about his work because he designed the field house at Swarthmore in 1933. He was cordial, and we had drinks with him, toured his house and heard about his latest project. This was the beginning of a long time friendship with Bud Greene and my admiration for Karcher, the man, and his Heath Road house which he designed around a living-room Adam mantle. This had been rescued from an old mansion which had been demolished in the Society Hill section of Philadelphia and given to him when he was just starting his practice.

It was a week or so after this visit (which I had not mentioned to Lucinda) that she told me that her realtor had shown her a house on Heath Road near the Bowman Avenue School. She said she liked the house, and, when she described it, I said that it sounded like the Karcher house. We then had the realtor arrange a tour and decided to buy the house. Mr. Karcher was planning to move into University City, The Fairfax, and he said we could move into Heath Road in the spring of 1952.

553 Heath Road

In the period 1951 – 1953, my teaching, research in the clinical investigation of potential useful drugs, and part time private practice, was done on a salary, as an employee of the School of Medicine of U of Pa. A retirement program sponsored by TIAA was offered by Penn in which I elected to participate. A monthly withdrawal out my salary was combined with a matching sum from Penn each month. Later, when I was no longer on salary, but in full time private practice, I continued the program by depositing the total monthly amount on my own. Based on advice given by Lucinda's friend, Quaker insurance salesman, Asa Way, life insurance policies with Northwestern Mutual were taken out in 1949, 1951, 1955, and a TIAA life policy in 1957. Today I know this was a prudent decision.

I was elected to the Pharmacology Society in 1949 and the
American Physiological Society in
1951 and I was able to participate
by making presentations in national
meetings. At this time in early 1952,
a Swiss physiologist, Aurelio
Cerletti was completing a year's
fellowship in the pharmacology
department at Penn. I first met him
at a social event of Professor and
Mrs. Schmidt. Cerletti was a
charmer and played jazz piano
beautifully. At this time he said he
planned to attend a meeting in
Cleveland where he would be
visiting with his chief, Ernest Rothlin of Sandoz Basel. I said I was
hoping to give a report at the same meeting. He said he would
introduce me to Professor Rothlin. He, too, was charming, a great
scientist, and business man. My good luck was that he and Cerletti
arranged for Lucinda and me to work in the Basel Sandoz lab
testing a new digitalis product on a dog heart-lung model. I was
able to get the support of Dr. Wolferth and Dr. Pepper. Soon I was
able to arrange a four month leave of absence with Dr. Fran Wood
and my immediate chief, William Jeffers.

Aurelio Cerletti

Lucinda and I arranged for a housekeeper to care for Joe, Tom,
and Mark. Just after Labor Day, we sailed from New York to Sout-
hampton on the Holland American line. The Sandoz representatives
in England arranged for me to visit Professor McMichael and
Professor Rosenheim at their hospitals in London. Both were
cardiologists. Then we went by channel train and boat to France,
staying in Paris for three days. While there, we met Dr. Ravdin,
from Penn, who happened to be staying for a day or two at the
same hotel that Sandoz had booked for us. We then took a high
speed train to Basel and were met by a Sandoz couple who took
us to our hotel on the north bank of the Rhine. This hotel was at
a point where the river flowed from east to west. The couple lived

on the same street and they were the couple who for three months made us most welcome.

Aurelio had arranged everything in preparing for the lab work and while there in an eight to nine week period we had 35 successful heart lung trials of the new Sandoz purified digitalis drug. On weekends, we used a Swiss Eurail pass and spent the weekend in a different part of Switzerland. After not too long it became obvious that Lucinda was expecting. This did not interfere with our social life during which we were often invited to dinner parties in private homes. About Thanksgiving time, Aurelio and I completed our project. One of his Italian associates helped us plan our trip through southern Switzerland where we visited Henry Sigerist, one of my History of Medicine professors at Hopkins, at his home in Lugano. We then went on to Venice and Rome where we had an audience with the Pope, Pacelli. We then went on to Naples and back to NYC on the "Independence," arriving back at 553 Heath Road about 15 December. The housekeeper was glad to see us as she found Joe, Tom, and Mark to be "busy bees."

After Christmas, I returned to the HUP and reported back to Dr. F.C. Wood, and told him what I had done. It was at this time that he asked me if I would head up the Department of Medicine teaching service at the Philadelphia General Hospital (PGH). He explained what he had in mind, i.e. teaching and arranging classes, on a full time

Visit To Rome

administrator's salary. I immediately recognized this as the end of my clinical investigation and part time private practice. However, I told him I would like to think it over and that I would give him my decision soon. Lucinda and I discussed it and she said she thought it was not the right step to take so I declined his offer a day or two later.

I was able to rejuvenate my research team. We were considering the study of more hypertensive patients with brain blood flows. Soon my chief, Dr. Jeffers, told me he was not going to authorize a renewal of the NIH research grant. This was no surprise. Before I left in September, Dr. Jeffers seemed to be more difficult, insecure, as if he was "out of the loop." Later he was found to have a an inoperable brain tumor and died in less than a year. He might have been trying to cooperate with Dr. Wood's PGH plan to have me work there. Lucinda and I shared these tribulations, which she remembered being part of her father's hospital life, even though he died in 1930, just as she was graduating Friends Central High School.

Ward Rounds on the Bortz Service

She and I were aware of the structural steel frame of the new Lankenau Hospital being built on Lancaster Pike, near our home in Merion. She knew our friend, Harrison Flippin was not only at HUP but also was on the Lankenau staff. She suggested I contact him. This I did and he arranged for me to have dinner with Lankenau's Board President, Alfred Putnam and his wife, along with Dr. Flippin. This went well and Mr. Putnam suggested that I meet with Dr. Bortz, chief of one of the medical services. Dr. Bortz, a past president of the AMA, was thought to be more progressive and possibly interested in my research background. Soon I was a member of the Bortz service and began (in the late spring of 1953) to make weekly "grand rounds" of that service at the old Lankenau in the city at Girard and Corinthian.

On April 27, 1953, after a short and uncomplicated labor, John Proctor arrived. His name was chosen by Lucinda, based on a book given by her late uncle Daniel Stackhouse. This told the story of the Stackhouse-Buchanan ancestor named John Proctor who fought in the French/Indian pre-revolutionary wars in western Pennsylvania. Lucinda was able to get an African-American woman, who was experienced in the care of newborns to be a "live-in" helper at 553 Heath Road. This was a big help and my parents helped in the financing of this helper and also a two week vacation in July 1953, at Barnegat Light, near the Coast Guard station and right on the beach. While I was there for a week, I bought a drawing pad and watercolor brushes and tried to create a beach scene with the lighthouse in the background. Lucinda upon seeing my rendition said, "Let me give it a try." Her effort was much better and that was the beginning of her lifelong hobby.

The technicians in my research group stayed on the payroll even

Christmas 1953

though we decided to analyze our data rather than to add to our series of brain blood flow measurements in hypertensive patients. These measurements were made before and after the patients' elevated pressure was lowered by several different drugs that were being studied for clinical application. Brain blood flow at the lower pressure levels was always in the normal range. These studies were published later in the Journal of Clinical Investigation.

After my vacation at Barnegat Light in July, I returned to the Hospital of the University of Pennsylvania. In August, I served as an attending on the Men's Medical Ward. When Dr. Wood, Department Chairman and chief of the cardiovascular section, returned from his vacation in September, he approved my working with Dr. Kay in the cardiology section. Dr. Sellers moved up in the hypertension section and reported to Dr. Jeffers, who was becoming more impaired. My office to see private patients was still on the third floor of the Maloney Clinic, although most of the cardiology group had moved to the 9ᵗʰ floor of the New Gates Building. My office there was quite small and not suitable for the examination of private patients. I had been invited to join an office group in the new Lankenau Medical Building with Dr. Miller and Earl Dougherty. Vincent Kling, the Hospital architect, was helping us with the plans for office space which he thought would be ready for occupancy in late 1954.

Joe and Tom were enjoying the Bowman Avenue School and we became active in the Home and School parent group. Later,

I served as a president of that group for a year. I learned that Dr. Clark Brown, chief pathologist at Lankenau, was willing to allow me to use two large rooms in the clinical laboratory part of the Hospital. I was able to secure the assistance of Dr. C. Riegel, who was Dr. Brown's chief of chemistry. She was willing to give some time to a potential research program using that space then not used. She and I worked out the details of a new grant application to the National Heart Institute for a cardiopulmonary research unit. I introduced my HUP technicians to her and was able to get Dr. Jerry E. Schmitthenner – just completing a medical residency at Lankenau – to head up the group with my direction. This was all approved by Dr. Ed Bortz. Dr. Hunter Neal also joined us. I was able to move all the equipment, which was lying idle in the hypertensive research rooms on the 9th floor at Gates – HUP out to the two rooms at Lankenau. This equipment had been purchased with federal funds and I cleared this move with NIH people before starting.

I was invited to become a member of the Merion American Legion Post which met in the Merion War Tribute House on Hazelhurst Avenue. I was interested in their summer golfing group. Each month, a golf club member would host the Legion golfers at his club. I became friendly with Bob Barker, an MIT alum, who was a member of Merion Golf Club as well as a successful business man in the city.

26th St. Barnegat Light

It was late in the summer of 1954 when Lucinda discovered a new house on 26th Street in Barnegat Light, two houses from the Atlantic beach, had come on the market. This was discussed with my parents and my mother arranged to send Lucinda $10,000 to buy it at the asking price. Soon afterwards, the Eckenhoffs were told of a house on 25th Street in the same block. They bought it and we were together there until 1965.

The research program sponsored by the National Heart Institute was under way in the cardio pulmonary unit with Dr. Schmitthenner devoting 85% of his time to this and perhaps 15% to Lankenau teaching – interns, residents, and Jefferson medical students. My work was 75% private practice, now in Suite 302 Lankenau Medical Building, with Doctors Malcolm Miller and Earl Dougherty. About 20% of my time was spent in supervising Dr. Schmitthenner and our two HUP technicians were under the tutelage of Dr. Riegel. She was devoting approximately 20% of her time in training these two women in new blood chemical tests that were not part of our HUP research program.

Our two oldest sons were then at the Bowman Avenue primary school and Mark was in the Merion Friends Meeting pre-school group. John was just beginning to walk and talk. Social activities were minimal, mostly with Lucinda's family, HUP colleagues, and our Heath Road neighbors including Stephen and Virginia Whelan, then on Baird

Summer at 26th St.

Road. Lucinda had been able to rearrange and furnish the house on 26th Street in Barnegat Light. The plan was to spend the summer there after school closed. This worked out well. My father came on and spent two weeks with us when I was there most of the last two weeks in July on my vacation.

My teaching at Penn was limited to Thursday mornings in the Cardiac Clinic followed by attendance at the weekly conference from 11:30 – 12:30. Our HUP technicians, one of which was Hannah Broomell, an alumna of Swarthmore, and a younger sister of my classmate G. Lupton Broomell, helped me to prepare the summary of our brain blood flow studies in 101 patients with essential hypertension. My co-authors were Carl Friedland and Charles Crumpton. The Journal of Clinical Investigation published this in 1954. Dr. Crumpton, after his return to Madison and the University Hospital, invited me to make a presentation to his medical staff colleagues at the hospital. This was published the same year in the Wisconsin Medical Journal.

The last study with my HUP colleagues was co-authored by my fellow HUP intern William T. Fitts. This was published in 1955 in the Transactions of the American College of Cardiology. Our first study at Lankenau was on nicotine's effects on cardiac work and coronary blood flow. This was presented in the spring of 1956 at the annual American Physiological Society meeting by Dr. Schmitthenner. This report led to a supporting grant from the Tobacco Institute Research Committee in mid 1956. This was chaired by Dr. C.C. Little, who had founded the Jackson Laboratory for Cancer Research in Bar Harbor, Maine earlier in his scientific career.

At the 1956
AMA Meeting

Lucinda was busy with our four sons; she managed all the finances, paying all the bills and hiring the help. When I would come home in the early evening, my most pleasant memory is that she would be playing the piano, with dinner all ready to be served immediately on my arrival. The older boys were being taught to cook, serve, and clean up. We tried to always eat our evening meal together as a family. Also she was getting better and better in her still life painting under Hobson Pittman. In 1958 we decided to join the Merion Golf Club and the boys started group lessons with Fred Austin. We also joined the Cynwyd Club and Norm Bramall tutored our sons in squash and tennis. That year I also was certified by written exam in NYC in internal medicine. There was great joy at 553 because this did not happen on the first attempt.

The cardiopulmonary unit research was doing well and the CIBA drug principals scheduled us a segment of their weekly medical show – called "Medical Horizons." Dr. Bortz seemed to be interested in our efforts and when, as a former President of the AMA, he was visiting hospitals in South Africa, he arranged for a young Afrikaner M.D. to have a year's fellowship with us at Lankenau. This he did on his own. However, he forgot to tell us about it. This offer we heard about only after the Potgeiters –

mother, their doctor father, and two boys, ages 6 and 8, had landed in NYC and called Dr. Bortz's office, when there was no one there to meet them. Dr. Schmitthenner volunteered to drive to NYC and we agreed to house them until a furnished house could be found, for they were planning to spend a year with us. Dr. Potgeiter was a good fellow, although he and his wife were heavy smokers. He was interested more in clinical cardiology and, although he helped us as with the animal studies, he really wanted to work with patients. When I was in South Africa in 1985, I learned he had died at a young age. In May 1959, Dr. Potgeiter made a presentation before the section on General Medicine of the College of Physicians of Philadelphia. This was on treadmill work capacity of patients with hypertension soon after myocardial infarction. This was published in the Transaction of the College that same year.

In the late spring of 1959, Lucinda accompanied me to the medical meeting in San Francisco. This related to our studies of Intravenous Synthetic Angiotensin in animals and patients (Hypertension – CIBA). Ciba pharmacologists were searching for a new director, to succeed Dr. Fritz Yonkman. Their representatives entertained us during the meeting. We extended our visit for three or four days in Palo Alto after the San Francisco meetings. We were reluctant to consider joining the CIBA group because Dr. Younkman had told me when alone in a private meeting, that he did not plan to retire. "I am being forced out." So my response was negative. Lucinda was surprised at all the blooms in the beautiful gardens in the better residential parts of Palo Alto, so early in the spring. She let me know that any time I wanted to move her to Palo Alto she was ready, and would have her suitcase packed.

Because of our presentations of the results of walking work capacity in recovery of patients by use of treadmill EKG (electrocardiograph), we were invited to attend a conference sponsored by the cardiologists of the University of Vermont at Burlington in August 1960. Before we left, I had lunch with Dr. Austin Lamont at HUP one of the Thursdays that I worked in the Cardiac Clinic. Our conversation covered the place of private boarding high schools for boys. He said that two of his sons went to Exeter in New Hampshire. Both "flunked out," but he said, "It's still the best." I told him about my plans to visit Vermont and New Hampshire after I attended the heart exercise meeting. He volunteered to write to Exeter a letter of introduction. This I accepted and gave him the details of my 14 and 13 year old sons. Lucinda contacted an older cousin, Becky Stackhouse, who lived in New Milford, Connecticut, near the Kent School. She invited us to spend the first days of our trip with her. This we did and visited Kent on the way to Burlington. There we were together with Dr. Zimmerman, formerly of Johnstown, PA and then at Cleveland City Hospital. We had a great time with him and his wife and enjoyed the exercise ECG meeting, realizing we were in on the start of these studies. Then we went to Exeter and then to Andover, and on the return trip, we visited Cold Spring, NY. From there we toured the campus of the West Point Military Academy.

Visiting the Andover Inn

After some urging, and with the support of the principal of the Bala Cynwyd Junior High, Joe completed applications to George School (where his Uncle Powell studied before going to Gettysburg College), Andover and Exeter. Joe was admitted to all three and, under some duress, chose Exeter. Lucinda and I drove Joe and Tom there in early September. Joe adjusted well enough and he was invited back for his second year. He graduated in 1964. It was on this trip that Lucinda made it clear to me that Exeter and Andover were not interested in an MD's list of publications, but expected him to be able to afford the "full package."

When, a few weeks after our return, I received my next bill for my space in Suite 302, which had increased considerably, I decided to explore having my own office in a building I owned. Knowing that a good location might be near a shopping center, I thought of a house near the Bala Cynwyd stores, on City Line, which had ample parking space. There were two Georgian style houses on St. Asaph's Road. One was owned by Dr. Babcock, a respected surgeon then retired from operating at Temple Hospital. The other was owned by Dr. Kimbrough who had just retired from his Pennsylvania Hospital Obstetrical practice. He was now heading the staff of the OB-GYN National Society in Chicago and living in an apartment there with his wife, while his two adult sons were occupying 13 St. Asaph's. On a visit, I met with Dr. Kimbrough and, in the autumn of 1960, made him an offer for his house. He said that the offer was so good he had to accept it.

In the background was the fact that although I was "not in the loop," I had heard that the Lankenau Hospital Board of Directors had a new chairman, Anthony Whitaker, Esq. of the law firm Morgan, Lewis and Bockus. There had been rumors that Miss Ethel Pew was encouraging administrative efforts

Joe and Lucinda at Exeter

to support a new Research Program at Lankenau. Miss Pew was financing the construction of a new building on the Overbrook Campus, with plans drawn by Vincent Kling. Our group had been contacted only as to what space, x-rays and other equipment might be needed. But that was only what we knew in December 1960, when the Norwegian MD, Dr. Rodahl appeared on the scene as the new Director of Research at Lankenau. Our team soon learned that he was there for "basic research," as his approach was not clinically oriented. So I was prepared to give up my projects and concentrate on private practice to be more in line with Lucinda's view of our #1 priority – i.e. education of our sons.

The situation came to a breaking point some time in the spring of 1961, when we had scheduled a patient study in the new x-ray room of the recently completed and furnished research building. We found that the locks had been changed and, not having the keys, we were unable to use the room. The patient study was cancelled and, after several meetings of our group, I went to the Hospital Director and told him that I had talked to the Director of the National Heart Institute in Bethesda reported to them that our studies were being obstructed and that our group had voted to return the remaining grant money. I never heard anything more after that.

13 St. Asaphs Road

Plans were made to rearrange the 13 St. Asaph house for 900 square feet of office space in the south east end of the building on the first floor. Harry McNichol, a contractor friend of Dr. S.T. Whelan's won the bid for the job. Work was started late in 1961. Malcolm Adam, the father of Addie Kirby, came to my help, offering me a salaried job as a cardiology consultant in the Penn Mutual HQ office – Washington Square, Philadelphia. Mr. Adam was then chairman of the board and Charles Tyson had just come on as president and a member of the board. Thus, I reduced the time I was in my office at Suite 302, cared for my hospitalized patients at Lankenau, and worked in the middle of the day at Penn Mutual. I examined prospects for high premium life coverage.

The work at St. Asaph continued from the autumn of 1961 into the winter and spring of 1962 and the office area was completed in April 1962. Lucinda hoped she could stay at 553 Heath Road. However, the Lower Merion Township Zoning Board denied my application to practice there without living on the premises. This was primarily due to the opposition of the Bala Cynwyd Property Owner's Association objecting to cars parking in a residentially zoned street. Reluctantly, in May/June Lucinda made plans to move into 13 St. Asaph's. She decided that she wanted to take the Adam mantle (trophy given us by Mr. Karcher, the builder/architect and previous owner) and the builder agreed to move it to the 13 St. Asaph living-room from 553 Heath Road. When that was done, that house was put up for sale and closure followed three months later. The first party in that living room, Lucinda invited all her relatives and a good time was had by all.

Lucinda had the landscape gardener work on the exterior, and flowering shrubs given to Dr. Kimbroh by grateful patients were fertilized and the rear garden lawn was reseeded. Soon it was late spring and time to get the 26th Street house at Barnegat Light ready for the summer. Lucinda arranged to go to Barnegat Light with two or three of the women in the Hobson Pittman painting group. This was in May, as I was responsible for the four boys, feeding, etc. The weekend passed and Lucinda returned with several new seascape pictures that she had produced. On my next trip, when school was out, we went to Barnegat Light to open the house and stock the larder. Lucinda asked me to take a walk with her north on the Atlantic beach. As we reached the 19th Street she pointed out a "For Sale" sign on top of high dunes. She suggested we go up along 19th Street and look at the lot. This was when I learned she had purchased the lot on her previous visit with her art group friends. I was then informed that a friend had suggested a local architect named George Daub. She had George look at the lot with her and discuss in a general way how the house might be sited. This is when I learned that the lot was not wide enough and that we had to acquire the vacant lot just south of us in order to get the architect to take on the job of designing the house. The owner of the lot next door was in the army and I learned he would be in Barnegat Light the next weekend. I made an appointment to talk to him about buying the lot. The next weekend I met with the owner and asked him whether he would sell and for how much. He told me and I paid his price. It turned out that I paid him more for the inside lot than Lucinda paid for the corner lot.

19th St. Barnegat Light

Mr. Daub was informed that there were now two lots for him to site the house and he agreed to take the job. I then learned that he was a patient of two of my mentors at the Hospital of the University of Pennsylvania, Dr. I. S. Roudin and W. T. Fitts. Lucinda had quite a time convincing Mr. Daub that she wanted the house her way and not his. Finally the plans were completed and, sometime in the early summer, he said it was time to put the job out for bids. The low bid was that of two fisherman-brothers (The Montgomerys) who did building in the off season. Daub suggested, that after his investigation of their previous work, he thought they should have the job. Work was to start that September. We spent that summer at 26th Street and the builders promised to have the house ready for occupancy the next summer.

In as much as my secretary, Elizabeth Albertson, had just moved (September 1962) to help me in my office at 13 St. Asaph's Road and new patients were few, I asked Mr. Adam if I could continue with my Penn Mutual work for another year. This was agreeable to the Medical Director (Bryan Dawber) and I agreed to have one of the physicians who had just joined the full time medical staff to work with me. The members of the Cardiopulmonary Unit team were on salaries for six months after the decision was made to stop our clinical and animal studies. Summaries were made for publication and those were completed with a video presentation to a general session of the American College of Physicians, then meeting in Atlantic City. The moderator was the Chief of our Medical Service, Malcolm Miller, with whom I shared space in S. 302. This was on 13 April 1962. The title was: "The Assessment of Physical Work Capacity in Coronary Disease." In the summer of 1962 Dr. Jerry Schmitthenner helped me complete a study of Lankenau Hospital Cardiac Clinic patients which was later published in the A. Journal of Cardiology-July 1965.

In 1963 I was practicing at 13 St. Asaph's and a garden party was held to which all my patients were invited. Lucinda made me this present, having been elected to the American College of Physicians at their annual meeting in Philadelphia. Although the builders of the 19th Street house were not speedy, and did not follow Daub's orders, they corrected whatever Lucinda asked them to do. We furnished and accepted the house the summer of 1963 and sold the 26th Street house. By Labor Day, Joe and Tom were on their way down east to their schools, Mark was in Bala Cynwyd and John was in Bala Primary.

My boyhood friend from Youngstown, Dr. Patrick, now an Obstetrician, wrote us saying he and Judy planned to visit us in Philadelphia. We were going to be in Barnegat Light over Labor

Day because this being the 50th anniversary of my parent's wedding we arranged to entertain my folks there. Beginning the day after my parents left to go back to Youngstown, Judy and Jim Patrick joined us, and together with Cary and Gary Garrison, then working with Del Monte in New Jersey. This was a fun weekend and we saw Judy and Jim only once or twice later.

Visit with My Parents

The autumn and winter of 1963 flew by and we were busy with practice at 13 St. Asaph's, and Penn Mutual, hospitalized patients at Lankenau, cardiac clinic and weekly rounds (Thursdays) with Dr. Wolforth early and the conference at noon at which he presided. He had guest speakers such as Dr. Bill Stroud, Dr. Sam Bellet and the surgeon Charles Bailey who was the Philadelphia pioneer cardiac surgeon. I did have time to apply to be certified as a sub-specialist in cardiovascular diseases by the American Board of Internal Medicine. My application was accepted and I reported to one of the hospitals in Houston on a beautiful April day. The exams were in the morning and although I did not know everything I was asked, I knew enough to be certified.

Lucinda was meeting with fellow art classmates weekly in the Philadelphia Museum of Art. Not long after I was back from Houston and very busy, Lucinda told me that a trip headed by Hobson Pittman-"Art Centers of Europe" was scheduled for late June the next summer (1964). Several of her closest friends were going to go and she said she was going and wanted me to be in charge for the approximately eight weeks she was to be abroad with that group. I agreed and she had a travel agent known as Mary Virginia Geyelin make arrangements. Mary Virginia was most cooperative and sent me all the info she had, allowing that she was still working on the details Hobson instructed her to arrange. Lucinda was getting advice from long time friends of Hobson who had negative experiences with him on earlier trips. Lucinda was determined to go and I agreed. I knew she would not let Hobson bother her and although I did not know him well, I proceeded to make the needed deposits.

About this time, early May 1964, I received an invitation from my friends in top positions at Sandoz, New York City to spend most of the day at Hanover, New Jersey, near Morristown where they were celebrating the opening of their newly built-USA Headquarters and Laboratories. Production was at various places in the USA and Europe. I accepted. My long time friends, Aurelio Cerletti, Carlo Henze and Rudi Bircher were there on a beautiful garden party day in mid May. When Cerletti heard about the trip Lucinda- 'Art Centers of Europe", he told us about the Swiss National Fair held only once every four years, which was to be staged in Lausanne on Lake Geneva the month of July. This featured the private collections of Swiss who had art of the post-Expressionist period. He seemed to know that the President of Sandoz, Professor Stoll was an art collector-whose private collection of Holder was outstanding. He had been asked by those in charge to submit some of his collection of art in that period. At that time he did not know what of Stoll's had been accepted. He did know that Stoll had a summer house in nearby Vevey and that he planned to be there all the time the fair was open to the public. Cerletti volunteered to ask Stoll whether we could visit him, as a group at Vevey. My response was: "You are a busy fellow, please don't bother." He said it would be a way of repaying Philadelphians for the good time he and his wife had in their only American home, 1951-52. I came back to Lucinda from Hanover very pleased to learn about the Swiss National Fair. I explained how we could arrange for our four sons to survive, if I left them the last two weeks in July in order to join the group in Lausanne.

The information about the Swiss Fair was passed on to Mary Virginia and I asked her to book me for a trip to Switzerland and the Netherlands and then on to the British Medical Association Annual Meeting in Manchester, England. When she told Hobson about the Swiss Fair, he asked her to see how it would fit into the itinerary he had in mind. Apparently it fit in for the next I heard it had been made one of the stops. It was only a few days later when I had a letter from Cerletti stating that Professor Stoll would like the group to be his guests at his Vevey house to see his collection on one of the two days in the last week in July. By this time I was on good terms with Mary Virginia and learned she was doing all the details as well. She was given Cerletti's letter and she picked out what she thought was the better day and replied with the tentative number, whose plans were definite. She sent me a copy of her letter and it was short and excellent.

1964 was the year that we were able to get Mark and John to accompany us to Exeter, picking up Tom at Andover so we could all be together for Joe's graduation. We have a picture taken by Lucinda by the river at Exeter with me and my sons in the foreground. It was on this trip that the brothers said they wanted to try to be at Barnegat Light by themselves, i.e. they did not want a housekeeper or a tutor. They did agree that if they were in trouble they would seek help from the Ostergrens who lived on the beach but across the road.

My secretary, Elizabeth Albertson, who was doing a wonderful job, was very good with patients, and kept my referring physicians informed about my schedule and how to reach me. She was a superb letter writer, correcting my grammar, and typing a perfect letter. I asked her advice about who I should try to get to cover me the weekends when I would be with my sons at Barnegat Light and when I was abroad the 3 to 4 weeks in Switzerland, The Hague, and Manchester. She said the patients liked Dr. Devine and she seemed to know that he was happy to fit in because he needed the extra money. I always paid him what the patients paid me in addition to a minimum if there were no calls. He and I worked this out in early June for the period until after Labor Day. Lucinda soon had the complete itinerary and it showed the departure by ship from NYC the last Saturday in June. I arranged to drive Lucinda and a friend to NYC in our heavy duty Buick station wagon.

Somehow, Miss Adams, a friend of Miss Pew, who decided not to join the group said she would go with me to NYC and keep me awake on the trip back to the Main Line. I had a warm feeling about the good humor of the attractive spinster, former social worker, then in her late 70s. So I agreed. After I returned her to her home in Bryn Mawr, I did some shopping as I planned to leave early

Sunday for Barnegat where Joe and his brothers had been all month. When I arrived at Barnegat Light I learned that they had a visitor. Apparently this was a friend of our architect, George Daub and his wife. He had told her about designing the house and wanted her to see it and write it up for the newspaper to which she sent her copy. Joe and Tom invited her in the house when she introduced herself as a friend of George Daub's. They gave her iced tea and cookies after they showed her both floors of the beach house and a "snow job" as they described it. The story was that their mother and father were on an art trip in Europe and they were in charge of Barnegat Light and Miss Albertson and Dr. Devine were in charge of my office and patients. They said they could shop, cook, and do the housekeeping as well as swim and sail. Joe was 18, Tom 17 and they had our Chevrolet station wagon as their wheels.

Picture from Bulletin Article

She wanted to know when and how she might reach me so she could "officially" report on the Daub house. I got a call from her Monday when I was back in the office at 13 St. Asaph's. She wanted permission to write a story that was more about the brothers than about the house. I told her to proceed: that if she had as good sense as George Daub, I could and would trust her. She wanted to bring a photographer and ask any questions of the brothers. The only stipulation to my yes was that she should interview all the boys at one gathering. The story she wrote was complimentary about the house the boys and their parents. It was published in the Evening Bulletin and we obtained enough copies so that it was put in several scrapbooks. The 4th of July celebration was great and when the Ostergrens entertained me I sought their help in watching what went on at "Surcease" (which was the name Lucinda had given our shore house.) Mary Virginia had worked out my itinerary and the boys drove me to the bus stop at Manahawkin in the late morning of the second Saturday in July. I got off the bus in NYC and took another bus to JFK to catch an overnight plane to Glasgow and a plane to Geneva. There, Sandoz people met me, took me through customs, and put me on the train to Lausanne. The group had arrived the previous day and was at the hotel where I was to stay with Lucinda. It was a great reunion with Lucinda and those I already knew. There was also a welcome letter to Hobson Pittman from Professor Stoll giving us the day, time and directions to his house.

The group explored the town, toured the lakefront and was enjoying the Swiss wines of that Canton. The visit to the Stoll house and their private collection was, as many said later, the high point of the trip. The day after the Stoll visit, we took the train and through Basel and spent the night at the Hague. The next day we visited the Van Gogh and saw the town. We then took the

Lucy on Vacation

train to Paris where the group was for 3 or 4 days. This was the only place where Pittman "over did it." He decided he wanted to go to the theatre and purchased tickets for the group without getting the assent of everybody. Only a few of us went and repaid Hobson. I never learned how this worked out. I think Lucinda might have paid Hobson for the tickets not used. I never asked!

My route to Manchester was by way of Amsterdam airport. This was a pleasant trip having said goodbye to Lucinda and the group as I was flying from Manchester to London and then Philadelphia. A week or so later I met Lucinda and the group as they flew home from London.

I received an invitation from my friends at Sandoz to spend a day there in September to report on Professor Stoll's reception and the viewing of his art collection at Vevey. Actually the meeting was to invite me to consider joining Sandoz as Medical Director of their San Francisco office. My decision was delayed pending discussions with John Y. Mace, my lawyer and Bill Duffel, my accountant as to salaries, bonus, moving expenses, as well as a trip to California to buy a house, etc. Several friends from Basel were scheduled to come to New York in December. I queried them about what new drugs Sandoz had in the pipeline. After the December outing I believed that there was "enough in the pipeline" to join.

In late December, Miss Albertson drafted a letter to my patients that I was giving up my practice 31 January 1965 and inquiring where I should forward their medical records. Sandoz agreed to pay Miss Albertson's salary so she could be at St. Asaph's until June 1, 1965 to close up my office and get patient records to the MD of their choice. Miss Albertson was then to become a Sandoz employee and be my secretary in San Francisco. They also agreed to pay all her moving expenses including her grand piano.

After February 1, 1965 I commuted from Bala Cynwyd to Hanover, NJ on Monday and stayed at a motel near their USA headquarters and returned to Lucinda on Fridays. Lucinda and I were flown to SF and spent several days looking at houses while staying in the Clift Hotel. After visiting Marin, Belvedere, San Francisco and Palo Alto, we decided on a house at 418 Palm Street, Palo Alto.

418 Palm Street

Plans were made for me to finish at Hanover in late June, have two weeks vacation with the family at Barnegat Light, and to drive west with Mark so that I could start work at 450 Sutter on 1 August. Lucinda, Joe, Tom and John remained at Barnegat Light. Joe left for his second year at Swarthmore and Tom joined him there for his freshman year. After returning from the summer at Barnegat Light, Lucinda and John were at 13th St Asaph's showing the furnished house to prospective buyers. Turnout was poor and, on the advice of her older cousin, she decided to make the arrangements with a mover to haul our furnishings to Palo Alto. Sandoz had agreed to pay for the move, so everything was crated and sent to California. John and Lucinda drove out to Palo Alto and surprised Mark and me with their arrival. Lucinda had not wanted to bother us until she was at 418 awaiting the arrival of the van. In mid September John was enrolled in Wilbur Junior High and Mark started in the 10th grade at Palo Alto Senior High.

In November I learned that my mother had an abdominal operation because of pain. At this procedure it was found that she had what was thought to be ovarian cancer with fluid in the abdomen and right thorax. The prognosis was poor. I arranged with my Chief at Sandoz Hanover, Dr. Carl Hemze, to come east via NYC and Hanover so he could update me on what was new there. My visit to Youngstown was brief. My mother knew she was dying; we kissed goodbye and I went to New York. Lucinda had promised to fly back to Youngstown after the funeral. My mother died on 7 December 1965. Lucinda flew back to Youngstown and arranged for my father to be with us in Palo Alto. She helped him pick out his favorite clothes and furnishings and arranged for a mover to haul them to Palo Alto. With the help of my Uncle, Frank Conroy, a realtor was selected to sell the house furnished at 1337 Fifth Avenue and their auto was given to Frank (still in the plumbing hardware store business when he was not doing musical chores.)

We were getting settled in Palo Alto at 418 Palm having had the Karcher Adam Mantle installed in the living room fireplace. After returning from my first visit to Sandoz, I became aware that the Swiss group in Basel had a different strategy for research and development than Henze and Bircher. I also noted some friction in the San Francisco office with

The Karcher Mantle

Harry Althouse. He was supposed to retire but he hadn't yet left. From other friends in industry, I heard that he was expressing negative views of my presence. I was also having difficulty with clinical investigators reneging on their agreements to start or finish projects that we had agreed upon.

I was commuting from 418 Palm to Palo Alto station and walking with Gary Garrison from SF station to 450 Sutter 5 days weekly. I would lunch after 1:30 PM and work out at the downtown Olympic Club. My father had his own room and bath in our house on the first floor off the kitchen. I was invited to join the Olympic Club by our insurance agent. The Garrisons, while working for Del Monte, had been in the Philippine Islands and Gary had been transferred back to be to the San Francisco headquarters. They were living in a house in Piedmont and looking for a larger house. Lucinda convinced them they should look at houses in Palo Alto and they selected one in the Crescent Park School area near us.

Lucinda and I were invited to visit Basel and meet with the scientists there and we did this in June 1966. Rudi Bircher met us at the train station. In Nov. 1966 Rudy Bircher's wife called to say he had a massive coronary and expired in the early morning. After trip to Basel for his memorial service, Hemze told me he was being moved out of his position to be Executive Director of the Sandoz Foundation (USA branch) in a NYC office and would be replaced by Doctor Albert Frey of Switzerland as head of Sandoz Pharmaceuticals at Hanover. My work continued with potential investigations with the assistance of Miss Albertson and two other secretaries who were there with Harry Althouse.

In the spring of 1967 I was alerted to the closing of the San Francisco office by Dr. Frey and the plan to move the operation back to Hanover. After discussing this with Lucinda, I decided to resign in order to remain in Palo Alto. Dr.Althouse, had introduced me to his friend David Rytand M.D., a cardiologist at Stanford, then chief of the outpatient cardiac clinic. I asked if I could be a volunteer worker in the clinic, and soon I was appointed to the staff and served there until I retired in 1984, and then became emeritus. I counseled with my lawyer and accountant. They advised me to challenge the change proposed, and, if necessary, to take legal action. This was relayed to Carlo Hemze, MD who had hired me, but was now out my division. He told me he would discuss the situation with the Chief Financial Officer at Hanover. A proposal was forthcoming that gave me a satisfactory separation (bonus and salary for two years in the future) which my advisors suggested I accept. By this time it was mid summer 1967 and I learned from George Houck, MD Chief of Student Health that he was retiring and that I might find a position there because the freshman class would soon be arriving on campus and would need to have their physical exams. I explored this with Dr. Hewitt Lee, Chief of MD hiring at the Palo Alto Medical Center (PAMC) and he told me, if I could pass the physical exam and supply a reference (David Rytand, MD) , I could start the Monday after Labor Day, 1967. I resigned from Sandoz on 31 Aug 1967 and began work shortly thereafter.

Through Dr. and Mrs. Houck, we met Dr. and Mrs. Grevatt. Dr. Grevatt was continuing to work at Stanford Student Health after Dr. Houck retired. He and I became friends and worked together, as well as playing tennis and socializing with our families. Ken played a great jazz piano and he was a prominent

With Ken Grevatt

asset to our dinner parties. They had five children and a pool at their house near the Menlo Country Club and our sons often joined their family at vacations.

The Garrisons

Lucinda was in touch with Carey Snow Garrison who was now living in Palo Alto. Lucinda had learned about the Palo Alto Art Club and began to meet with the amateur artists there. Flora Houck introduced her to members of the Palo Alto Garden Club and the Palo Alto Medical Doctor's wives group. At one of those sessions she met the wife of an orthopedic doctor who was interested in landscape watercolors and suggested that Lucinda join that group. They painted in the Portola Valley area. One evening at dinner, Lucinda told me she was attracted to the foothill home sites, and, inasmuch as I no longer had to commute to SF, would I consider moving to

Portola Valley? I said, "Let's do it" and she said she would start looking for houses. It seemed only a week or so later that she announced that she had found a place she liked and requested I visit it with her the next Saturday morning. The house was located at 380 Golden Oak Drive in Portola Valley. After seeing it, I agreed that we should make an offer.

In the academic year 1967-1968, Joe and Tom were at Swarthmore. Mark was slated to graduate from Palo Alto Senior High in June and had taken College Boards. He was admitted to University of California at Santa Barbara where several of his Santa Cruz surfing friends were planning to attend. Mark had also been admitted to Swarthmore thanks to the assistance of the Dean of Admissions, Fred Hargadon, and was challenged by us to join his brothers there rather than going to Santa Barbara. John was in his last year at Jordan Junior High and, having had a motorbike accident, became more interested in autos. His mother bought him a VW while we were living in Palo Alto. My father, aged 87 was still living with us at 418 Palm. We were aware that he might need more attention then what Lucinda and I were able to give him. To get a baseline, I asked Dr. Felsovanji, a Hopkins classmate of mine, if he would examine him and formulate a program of care. Lucinda knew of a caregiver who was in the East Palo Alto area and had a vacancy. This is how my father, in early autumn of 1968, was moved into his own apartment in Palo Alto.

I was working at Stanford Student Health which was under the direction of Dr. James McClenahan, a temporary Chief picked by President Sterling. He had scheduled conferences with each of his staff. When I met with him, shortly after starting there, he asked if there was anything that he might be able to do for me. I responded by saying that Dr. Rytand, then Chief of Cardiology, had told me that I might work in Cardiac Clinic when a suitable schedule could be implemented. Now that Dr. Shumway was starting his study of cardiac transplantation after the pioneer work of Bernard in South Africa, the candidates were being evaluated in the Cardiac Clinic. I asked if I could spend 3 to 4 hours weekly in the Cardiac Clinic if that was agreeable to Dr. Rytand. Dr. McClenahan agreed to try to arrange that and asked if I had any other requests. I said I understood that certain members of the Stanford Volunteer Faculty, who were interested in golf, might have the privilege of playing in the Stanford University Golf Course as members of the Stanford University Golf Club. Dr. McClenahan said he was not aware of that but he knew Fred Glover in President Sterlings staff and he would inquire about it. Soon after, I was invited to become a member of the Stanford Golf Club and the Stanford Faculty Club. Dr. McClenahan said I could spend 4 to 8 hours per week working in the Cardiac Clinic in the afternoons and on weekdays when he had staff to cover my absence. This was arranged and I began working in the Cardiac Clinic in the autumn of 1968.

Joe III had graduated from Swarthmore in June 1968. Lucinda and I had attended his graduation and were staying with Aunt Alice Snow in Wallingford. We were on our way to Europe to participate in the post graduate program "Medical Centers of Europe" which had been arranged before I joined PAMC and agreed to by them. John had

My Father at Golden Oak Drive

convinced his mother that the Palo Alto Mercedes dealership had a good deal to buy a new Mercedes and pick it up at the factory near Frankfurt. This we did, going from Joe's graduation to the Philadelphia airport, and flying from JFK nonstop to Frankfurt. While in Europe we visited friends in Bavaria and Switzerland and traveled to Vienna, Bari, and, Padua before returning the car to Germany to be shipped to San Francisco. The car was in Palo Alto within two weeks of our return there in early September. Joe III had worked the summer of 1968 at Rolling Green Golf Club in Springfield and decided he should go to business school. He applied, and was admitted to UC Berkeley Business School. Tom was in his final year at Swarthmore. He had majored in Art History and had taken the required pre-med courses. As the academic year began, he was exploring what medical schools he should consider.

In early 1968, Lucinda made an offer on the Portola Valley property for $68,000. We had received an offer of $95,000 for our

Palo Alto house with an early (September 1969) occupancy. The 380 Golden Oak house would be available before then and the deal was closed.

Tom graduated from Swarthmore in June 1969 and decided to go to UCLA Medical School. The Dean of Admissions (who had a fellowship in Gastroenterology at Penn in the early 50's) wrote me that he was happy to have an Art History major in his 1st year group with an Andover/Swarthmore and family-medical background.

We learned from Lucinda's brother, Powell, that he would be on a sabbatical in Cardiff, Wales the autumn of '68 and he asked if we would take their son, John, into our house. We agreed and John Thomas and John Proctor began at Woodside High that fall. Although John Thomas bought a car as soon as he arrived in California, Lucinda had the previous owner take the car back, chiefly because John did not have a driver's license in California.

The house on Golden Oak Drive was close to Patsy and Joseph Whiteley, friends of Lucinda's, at Buck Hill Falls in the early '30s. Soon after we moved into 380 Golden Oak Drive, Tony Felsovanyi told me his wife, Nancy, was terminally ill with breast cancer and asked if I might be interested in being a locum tenens in his office while he spent more time with his wife. I agreed with the understanding that any new patients I had would be mine, and, thus, started again in private practice. After 3 months, I moved into space with Dr. Guterman and had a 20 family nucleus of patients. Eventually, I had an opportunity in late 1969 to share space with Dr. John Milburn in his office at The Medical Plaza, 1101 Welch Road, Palo Alto, near the Stanford Hospital which was closer to our home in Portola Valley. There I remained until I accepted the offer to serve as a consultant to the Department of Health of California seeing patients at Agnews. In 1978 I joined the medical staff of the Menlo Park VA Hospital where I cared for the acutely ill patients on the medical ward until I retired 31 Dec 1983. In 1984, I retired from Stanford as an Emeritus Clinical Associate Professor of Medicine. My work as a volunteer teacher at Stanford was: Clinical Instructor in Medicine, 1967-1969 and later, Associate Clinical Professor of Medicine.

Mark was thriving at Swarthmore where he majored in Art History, and played soccer and lacrosse. He was made a co-captain of the lacrosse team in his senior year and graduated in 1972. John graduated from Woodside High in 1971 and entered Swarthmore as an Engineering major. He had also been admitted to U.C. Berkeley but he was convinced by his brothers to go to Swarthmore.

After moving to Golden Oak Drive, Lucinda continued her association with the Palo Alto Garden Club. Lucinda stayed with this group and was one of the representatives when volunteers were asked to serve as docents when Filoli was turned over to the National Trust. One of the highlights of our stay at 380 was a Sunday afternoon Garden Party featuring some of Lucinda's and Mrs. Austin's works. I remember that Addie Adams Kirby Sharples came to the party on a beautiful Sunday afternoon.

Mark graduated in 1972. That summer he did odd jobs, such as mucking out stables in Portola Valley. His motorcycle was stolen from the apartment in South Palo Alto he was sharing with surfer friends. Because we felt he lacked direction, we decided to consult Carl Garrison, a professional ranch manager who was then president of the Alumni Association of the UC Davis agricultural school. Mark was interviewed by key professors and admissions officers at Davis and was admitted on a trial basis but did well in the science courses. He was able to earn a Master's Degree in two years, i.e. 1974. After working on private ranches until 1977, he was offered a job working with the BLM in Meeker, Colorado. Mark is still there as I write this in April 2005. John, after a trial at UC Riverside, went back to Swarthmore and earned his degree as a member of the class of 1975. After Tom finished at Swarthmore, he went to UCLA School of Medicine and graduated in 1973. Following post graduate training in Internal Medicine and Emergency Medicine, he joined a six man group in the Santa Clara Valley Medical Center. He is still with that group.

Joe after receiving his MBA from Berkeley started in the Bureau of Labor Statistics in Occupational Health and Safety. After a few years there, he obtained a job with the Research Department of the Telephone Workers Union. While there, he was appointed to the President's Commission on noise-level standards. He wrote the minority report stating the case for a lowering of the allowable decibel levels to prevent hearing loss. This brought him to the attention of a San Jose MD who the Governor, Jerry Brown, had appointed as his Director of Health. As a result of this Joe was offered a position in the Dept. of Health and he and his new wife moved to Sacramento.

Lucinda was the major influence on her sons' character formation, educational standards, and healthy living styles. She gave monetary rewards for not smoking, which she, herself, had given up before our marriage in July 1942. She encouraged them in art and music and in their professional careers. When John came home from high school each day she was there to meet him. She brought him a used Volkswagen when we were in Palo Alto in 1966 and he was instrumental in choosing the Mercedes in 1968 and picking out the Porsche 911 I bought her for her birthday in 1971.

Lucinda was a gregarious individual and became a member of a woman's group in Alpine Hills, later serving as its president. Our closest friends in California were probably Cary and Gary Garrison.

We had moved to Portola Valley chiefly because of her long-time friends, the Whitelys from her summer days at the Buck Hill Inn. She particularly liked Dr. Ken Grevatt whom we met because of George and Flora Houck. They had been responsible for Ken coming to Palo Alto from Santa Barbara to work at Stanford Student Health. Lucinda loved to give parties during which Ken Grevatt would play piano. Patty and David Jacobson were usually in attendance as well as Homer and Helen Hunt. Lucinda and Helen did the work at the print table for the Stanford Committee for Art every 2nd year fund raiser. Tom and Renata Sharples, who we had met through Philadelphia friends, were also always invited. Renata played the piano well and helped Lucinda pick out the baby grand that graced the 380 living room.

Lucinda also possessed a great deal of business acumen. She was fortunate to share with her cousins the estate of her grandfather Stackhouse and her father's Life Insurance trust. She sought professional advisors but mostly she liked Tom Sharple's ideas of what to have in her portfolio. Coming to California, a joint property state, we were aware that we should do something about having her separate property segregated. We had several accountants in California but it was not until we moved to 380 and titled the house in both names that we decided to seek help. Our friends, the Whitelys, put us in touch with their neighbor, John Wilson, Esq. who had an office in Palo Alto. Bob Greene, a nephew of Brydon S. (Bud) Greene, put us in touch with an accountant in San Francisco, named Bonnie L. Ripple. In 1981, Wilson and Rosati, with the help of Bonnie Ripple, set up the Lucinda T. Hafkenschiel Trust.

My father was in his own apartment and at that time had a "caregiver", a practical nurse who looked in on him and several other elderly residents in the same apartment complex. About 1 August, his caregiver found him short of breath and with chest pain. Dr. Guterman was called and went to his apartment. After examining him, he called for an ambulance and had him admitted to the Hoover Pavilion of the Stanford Hospital. The diagnosis was an acute coronary with pulmonary edema. I was making morning rounds and, when I got back to my Medical Plaza office, I received a message from Dr. Guterman that the ECG and enzymes had confirmed the diagnosis of heart muscle damage and that my 89 year old father was conscious, more comfortable and seemed to be responding to treatment for pulmonary edema. After I cared for the two patients on my schedule, I went to his room in Hoover. He greeted me saying only that he had a bad night. I saw him again later that day. When I saw him early the next morning he said he had another bad night, thinking he was a "goner." I reassured him but Dr. Guterman was skeptical that he would survive as a portable chest x-ray showed heart enlargement and fluid in both lung bases. I went to my office and two hours later I received a message that he died soon after I had seen him. He had agreed to give his body to the Medical School at the University of California. No funeral was held.

Lucinda and I had planned to attend a medical meeting in Honolulu two days after his death, and we decided to go through with our plans. It was a wonderful five-day break in our routine and we decided that we would do it again now that I was my own "boss" and we were both in good health. In the years between 1971 and

1978, we traveled to Italy, Egypt, the Greek Islands, Tokyo, Hong Kong, Bangkok, Rangoon and Taiwan, and Indonesia. In 1977 we stayed at "Domus Medicus" in London, as a member of the Royal Society of Medicine and then drove on a road trip to Oxford, Blenheim and Wales. We left our car at the ferry and went on to Ireland and Scotland, taking the train down the east coast from Edinburgh to London.

In 1978, I accepted the invitation to join as a Medical Consultant in the Menlo Park Division of the VA Hospital. Lucinda and I had already booked a trip to New Zealand, Australia and Fiji going west through the Hawaiian Islands in November 1978. It was a great experience and Lucinda decided to stay for 7 to 10 days in Kauai on our return trip. She was looked after while there by Tom's friend and roommate at UCLA, John Black, who was in dental practice on Kauai.

The next year, we learned that Mary Sewall Hyde and her husband, Lewis would be in the Ladera neighborhood visiting their daughter, Jane Williams, and her husband. Jane was in the investment planning business and we introduced her to Joe and Tom. The Hydes stayed long enough for us to entertain them at 380 with a dinner party. At that time, they told us about a trip that they were planning to take to Pakistan, Kashmir, Nepal and India. Lucinda was interested in joining them and we arranged to travel with the Hydes the next winter. The trip went well but, when we arrived home, Lucinda was aware that she had intestinal problems which she attributed to the Lomotil we had taken while in India. My physician friend, Richard Babb, at the Palo Alto Clinic examined her by colonoscopy and large bowel x-rays and uncovered a mass in her pelvis the size of a grapefruit. She was operated on in May 1982 and the surgeon told me that her situation was inoperable because of what seemed to be ovarian cancer with fluid and metastases in the abdominal cavity. He recommended chemotherapy which she accepted. By July she was in remission and we traveled to Meeker that month to see our son Mark. After returning home, she complained of right upper abdominal pain and this was found to be an enlarged liver. She underwent another abdominal operation and the surgeon was able to remove the tumor in the pelvis but the metastases in the liver were not touched. By Christmas 1982 she was under morphine therapy and she was admitted to Stanford Hospital for the last week of her life, dying on January 16, 1983. Post mortem examination confirmed the diagnosis of cancer in the ovary. No service was held, at her request. Her ashes were spread at the home she loved in Portola Valley and at Mark's acreage at Meeker. I continued working at the Menlo Park VA until December 31, 1983, and then retired.

7.   The Test of Resiliency Period: 1984

I had the good fortune to be the medical officer in charge of the acute medical wards of the extended care service at the Menlo VA before Lucinda died. This association was the major factor in my ability to resume my responsibilities the next Monday morning after her death. This association had begun 1 June 1978 and continued until I retired 31 December 1983.

During that period, I reported each week day at 0800, cared for the acutely ill patients who were transferred there the previous day because of behavior and medical/psychiatric problems in a "locked ward" setting supervised by MD psychiatrists and psychiatric nurses. I did not miss a day of duty because of illness or family problems and the other physicians and nurses were most supportive for my efforts after Lucinda was diagnosed in May 1982.

My recollection of how I happened to join this VA Hospital staff relates to the pattern of continuing medical education I was following while having a private practice at the Medical Plaza, 1101 Welch Road, Palo Alto. I supplemented my practice by being a medical consultant to the State of California Hospital system/ Agnews Hospital in Milpitas, CA, a twenty five minute drive from Palo Alto, and aiding and assisting the San Francisco office of the Veterans' Administration in claims decisions. This was a one hour drive each way. The Department of Medicine of Stanford Hospital had "grand rounds" every Thursday morning. The chief at that time was Dr. Halstead Holman. As a staff member, I attended those "rounds" and, over the period of time from 1966 to 1978, I met and knew something about most of the regular attendees.

One physician, whom I sat next to, was Harvey Blume, a graduate of Stanford Medical School. He knew about my part-time association with the San Francisco VA claims department. Sometime early in May 1978, he casually suggested that he would like to have me join this Internal Medicine Group on the Menlo Park Campus. This was because this World War I facility was being modernized and the census of the permanent patients would be increasing. At the time I was aware that my office patients were mostly in the Medicare age bracket and that I was not being reimbursed adequately for the time I spent with them, my net was declining at a time when we wanted to travel. I asked Dr. Blume what the duties would be. He explained those and told me what the salary and benefits would be for the entering civil service level. I knew that my military service and fellowship in cardiology at Penn for one year, gave me almost five years of federal service, so, the possibility of a Federal Civil Service pension benefit was another consideration. Another advantage was that there would be no night duty. At that time, our only education financial load was our son, John, who was then back at Swarthmore, I concluded that it was a "win/win" situation. As a result I closed my 1101 Welch Road Office.

Cynthia was expecting during Lucinda's troubles and shared her concern with Lucinda as to what she should name her expected daughter. Out of the names Cynthia suggested, my recall is that Lucinda's choice was Erin. In September of 1983 Tom and Wendy were married in London. This was arranged as part of a trip to England and Italy. A reception to celebrate their marriage was hosted at their home in Portola Valley by me and the bride's father, Fred Hassett. My social life was widened by being introduced at dinner parties in Portola Valley hosted by Pat Crooks and Joe Whitley and also Jane Langhorne and her husband, Keene, who was a retired Pan AM pilot. Also in this group were Elizabeth Higgins and her husband Wilson Todd, then living in Palo Alto.

The Gribbons, when they were told of our 1965 move to Palo Alto, had suggested to us that we should be in touch with Pat McNair and her husband, David Jacobsen. David was an administrator and legal advisor to Stanford University President, Wallace Sterling.

In January 1984 I took a trip with a physicians seminar group to the Antarctic Peninsula by way of Miami, Santiago, Chile and the Falklands. The group (10 MD's) traveling on the Salen Linblad "Polaris" was lead by a psychiatrist on the staff of Columbia University Medical School, and the seminar was publicized as part of the continuing medical education program of the AMA. My family helped me assemble special clothing such as boots, long underwear, and a parka. The flight from San Francisco to Miami was uneventful as was the flight from Miami to Santiago on Air Chile. However, when I looked for my bags, (which I had checked thru), the bags with my winter clothing were not there. Because we were only to be in Santiago overnight, and would be flying south to the Chilean Port in the morning, I was resigned to the fact that I probably would not see my bags for the remainder of the trip which is exactly what happened.

However, on the "Polaris" Mike, the Australian leader of the expedition, having dealt with similar problems in the past, reassured me that I would be adequately outfitted. I was told to meet him after breakfast the next morning and he would outfit me. This he did. His storeroom was large and many outfits had been given to him by previous adventurers who had not wanted to carry the heavy clothing home with them. I gave him a large tip at trip's end which is probably why I have been on his mailing list for exotic adventure trips around "remote" places in the world ever since. He had made contacts with all the research stations in the Antarctic area and had done many favors for the people there over the years. As a result the scientists made themselves available for interviews by our groups of physicians, wives, and traveling companions. What we learned was that they often dealt with by excess intake of alcohol and calories. This resulted in divorces but no suicides, and much mental illness but generally not the irreversible type. I visited the stations by zodiac, swam in several hot pools on the beach, and took many pictures with my Leica. Also I collected stamps of different countries which I believed might be of interest to Erin, and which I sent to her when I returned to California. I visited the British, French, German, Russian, and US Research stations. On return back to the US, I retrieved my lost luggage in Santiago.

I had read in the bulletin of the college of Physicians of Philadelphia the obituary of Alexander Rush, M.D. I knew he had married Carol Mac Donald Smith in September 1945. After reading the obituary, I tried unsuccessfully to reach Carol by phone on several occasions. I had been invited to a dinner party in Burlingame. At the dinner table, the hostess, Maria, sat me next to an attractive woman who said she lived in San Francisco and knew my hostess date, only as a member of the club. To make conversation, she said: "What is important to you at this time?" I looked at her, and evidently, she was expecting a reply. So I said I learned that a woman I dated in 1942 while an intern at HUP, had just lost her husband in Philadelphia. I had been unable to contact her by phone and I thought it important to do so because I was planning on going to Philadelphia in April for the opening day events at Merion Golf Club, and wanted to visit her. She asked, "What's her name and why do you want to call her." I said her name was Carol Smith Rush and that, as a 21 year old in 1942 she was most attractive and mature, and was now a widow.

She said, "I have a friend in San Francisco who is married to a Rush from Philadelphia. I would be surprised if I could not get her address and phone number from my friend's husband. If you will be available, I will call you tomorrow and tell you what I have learned". I said, "Great," and believed she would do what she suggested. The next day I stayed home all morning and, just before noon on Saturday, she called with Carol's number and home address. I was pleasantly surprised. I called several times but there was no answer and no message machine. I tried several more times without success. The next Saturday I resolved to spend more time calling again if there was no answer. Late that evening I did get an answer and talked to Carol. She was pleasant but reserved. I asked if I might call her again and she allowed that I might.

Later, I learned that one of her good friend's husband, Tom Langfitt, had celebrated a birthday that day, and she had attended a celebration and was exhausted by the time I talked to her at eleven p.m. that evening. Later in April, 1984 I learned that Carol's friendship with Tom began when he was the Senior Resident in Neurosurgery at Hopkins Hospital. He had assisted Carol's surgeon, Dr. Chambers, in 1960 in removing two tumors that deadened her 8th nerve nucleus. Carol made a great recovery but had a residual ptosis, (droopy right eyelid), complete loss of hearing in the right ear, and impaired balance so that she had difficulty riding a bicycle. I received a call last evening that Tom died on Aug. 7, 2005. He had lost 40 to 50 pounds over the prior 6 months and, after extensive testing at the Hospital of University of Pennsylvania, was found to have miliary tuberculosis. He did not respond to treatment, became more depressed, and refused to take medications or eat. After a week of hospice care, he expired.

After several phone conversations, Carol asked me if I might be the HUP intern that she invited to go to the circus with her on a Friday afternoon in February or March in 1942. I responded that I was, indeed, that intern. I told her that I was going to be in Philadelphia the last week in April. She said she had already planned to go to Vienna, Austria where her younger daughter and her husband would be on a "pony trekking" trip. She told me her mother still lived at the same address on Lesley Road where I stayed when I had dated her in early 1942. I told her I would try to visit her mother while I was in the area. I went to Merion Golf Club and, after playing, staying tried to call Mrs. Hollingsworth, however her staff would not allow her to come to the phone. I later learned she had "shingles" involving her left eye. Soon after that she had a stroke, and became severely disabled. She was then 94 but lived to be 101, dying on New Year's Eve in 1990. Unable to see Mrs. Hollingsworth, I returned to California.

Preparing Golden Oak for Sale 1984

When I arrived home I found that the Salen Lindblad tour leader had written me about a trip on the Baltic in the "Polaris", with a tour of the Hermitage Museum, as the featured event. I was particularly interested in some Manet paintings there that I had seen in one of Lucinda's museum brochures. In the back of my mind was the idea that if I ever had a chance to go Leningrad I wanted to see the Impressionist collection in the Hermitage. I replied to the Baltic trip announcement, asking for more information. This information I had received but I had made no decision before 1 May 1984.

On my return from Philadelphia I found I had also received a phone message from Joanna des Pres. She had learned about a Bergen "mail boat" trip around "The North Cape", which was part of the Norwegian Government's way of providing mail and freight service to remote coastal villages. She indicated that she had been invited by an old friend living in Paris to use their Paris apartment after the Norway trip and was inviting me to join her. It was then that I decided to book on the Polaris which was sailing from Copenhagen after the proposed trips to Norway and France. I told Joanna I would go if I could pay my own way.

The trip was a great experience and there was time for me to write a postcard to Carol in Villanova nearly every day. I arrived back in the US in early August and stayed in Merion with Dr. and Mrs. S.T. Whelan who were holding mail for me. One of the letters I received there was from Carol inviting me to visit her at her house "Woodlark" in Northeast Harbor, Maine. I was using a rental car to get around in Philadelphia and planning to fly back to Portola Valley. John Proctor was checking my mail and paying any bills. After a phone call to John, I decided to delay my return for another 14 days in order to be able to accept Carol's invitation to Maine. John urged me to do whatever I wished to do. So I began to explore the details of going to Maine. The only question was how to get there.

I decided to drive. With a 5 AM start from the Whelans, I made the 600 mile trip in 11 hours. I arrived at 11 Harborside Road in Northeast Harbor, Maine at 1630. Carol greeted me cordially and said I just had time to shower and change my shirt as the neighbors had invited us for drinks at 5:30. We walked a short distance to the house of the Millers, a retired couple from north Jersey who owned a large three story house built in 1890. The visit was very pleasant. After cocktail hour, Carol indicated that she had a reservation for 7PM at her favorite restaurant in Bar Harbor which was 10 miles to the east. The food at "Georges" was delicious and the service was excellent. We talked on our return to 11 Harborside and, after an hour, I retired, exhausted from my long day. When I arose the next day at 7 Carol was already up and had breakfast ready. We walked to the village grocery store and Carol bought a few items. She had arranged for us to go to the harbor at 11 to board Billy Lippincott's power boat for a picnic lunch near Cranberry Island. Billy was a former Princeton Dean and active in the island A.A. group. His wife was much younger and a talented artist. We returned at about 3 PM and Carol and I enjoyed a simple but adequate dinner at 7. During dinner Carol talked about what she did in Maine and what her social life was like while she was there. I told her I had to leave early the next morning to get back to the Whelan's house before dark.

I was able to get on my scheduled flight the next day and spent the trip thinking about what I would do, when, and if, Carol decided to accept my offer to have her visit me in California. She seemed pleased that I had invited her but nothing definite was decided as to when, or for how long, she would stay. I told the Whelans that I would be returning to Philadelphia; but to court Carol, not Martha. What I liked about her was her low-key, outgoing manner. She said, "I know all about myself, I want to know about you." It was the third week in August when I arrived at 380 Golden Oak and John had managed the house and my correspondence well. Joanna was not at all pleased with my summer adventures after I left her. John was proceeding on his quest to get another try at the Economics Department orals so he might qualify for his B.A, at Swarthmore.

My next trip was to Philadelphia in late September to play in the Merion Golf R.T. Jones Jr. Memorial Tournament. I accepted the 1984 invitation and I made a reservation to stay the weekend at the St. David's Hotel not far from Carol's house at 870 Lesley in the Ithan area of Villanova. Early in the morning of the last Thursday in September I arrived at the Philadelphia airport, rented a car, and drove to Carol's house. She was having breakfast and I joined her for coffee. I told her that I had a room at the St. David's Hotel and was going to check in there and unpack my clubs so I could use the Merion Golf practice range. She said, "I have your room all arranged for you. Stay here. Call the hotel and cancel." This is what I did. I unpacked, went to the golf range, and had lunch at Merion finding out the details of the next day's (Friday) event. Then I went back to Carol's house, talked, and I had a siesta. When I awakened Carol was preparing dinner. We had drinks, finished dinner, and I retired early.

Friday morning was sunny. After breakfast with Carol, I went to Merion for the competition. This was followed by drinks and dinner. I returned to Carol's house and we had wine and talked for several hours. The next morning I had a hearty breakfast and told Carol about a trip that I was exploring which was to join Gary Player and his wife who were hosting a group of golfers to play in South Africa the next February. I said I wanted to marry and if she would agree, I would arrange for our honeymoon to be the golf trip. I asked if she would come to California in the next four to eight weeks to meet my sons. This was worked out for November and she arrived in Portola Valley the Monday of election week. I was working in the polls the next day and arranged for two of Lucinda's friends, Helen Harmon and Mrs. Michener to come to 380 Golden Oak after an early breakfast. They entertained Carol for the day. All went well and all four of my sons arrived that weekend and met Carol. We had a tailgate party on the Stanford campus before the USC football game and went out to dinner together after the game. Their acceptance of Carol was enthusiastic and she was introduced to other friends before she returned to 870 Lesley's.

Before she left she asked me to come to 870 Lesley for Thanksgiving. Although she had a commitment to be with the Page house party in the Bahamas, she had arranged with her widowed sister, Ginny, to look out for me until she returned. I accepted. Ginny and I played golf at Gulph Mills, lunching was with several of their friends and Ginny had me for

Stanford Tailgate Party

dinner at her house, driving me everywhere as I did not have a car. Carol had left the kitchen at 870 Lesley well-stocked and made it clear that she wanted me to stay with her until I had met both of her daughters, the older living in Kalamazoo and the younger, an architect, living in Madrid. This daughter was expecting twins in May, and was coming to 870 Lesley after Christmas. This plan was a surprise to me and I returned to Portola Valley. There I consulted my pastor, Father George Thomas, at "Our Lady of The Wayside" as to how I should proceed in marrying a Protestant. I was able to get Carol to come to California before we left for Kalamazoo on Christmas week. We were invited to spend Christmas with Dr. and Mrs. William Purdy. Carol and I had at least two interviews with Father Thomas in mid December and he was able to find out from Carol what the nearest parish was to Carol's home in Villanova. This was St. Katherines in Wayne and Carol was able to give Father Thomas the name of the Pastor and his mailing address. Father Thomas wrote this priest saying that I was a "long time" (15 plus years) parishioner and that he approved the marriage.

After Christmas I returned to 870 Lesley to be with Carol, who was awaiting the arrival of daughter Sandra. Her husband, Martin, was staying in Madrid. It was at that time I phoned the Pastor of St. Katherine's, Wayne. He welcomed me to the Philadelphia area and said he had received Father Thomas' information about me. He inquired what church Carol attended and I told him St. David's, the Episcopal Church. He replied that he knew all the clergymen and their work on marriage was always pleasant. He suggested I do whatever Carol and her pastor desired.

Carol and I met at St. David's with Reverend Rudi Moore, the minister that Carol liked the best. He had presided at Dr. Rush Memorial Service in October 1983 and Carol was most appreciative of how he had conducted that service. Sandra arrived in early January and Carol told her we were to be married on 25 January. Sandra arranged to stay with her sister Mollie and her family when they came to be with us at 870 Lesley Road for the Friday wedding. Cynthia and Joe came with Erin. Mark came from Meeker, Colorado and stayed at Carol's mother's house. Steve and Terry Whelan were at the morning ceremony along with Carol's sister Ginny, and Lee and Bobby Taylor. We then had dinner together at 870 Lesley Road where we were joined by the Langfitts.

8. Philadelphia Revisited: 1985 To 2005

After our marriage on January 25th at St. Davids in Radnor and, with the holiday parties behind us, we prepared for our trip to visit the Rodman Pages on Exuma in the Bahamas. I had told Carol I wanted to have her join the Gary Player tour of South Africa golfing venues in late February. There was a possible golf outing in Rio, Brazil and we decided to do that after Exuma. At the Pages, we were joined by the Chews and the Starrs. We flew from the Bahamas back to Fort Lauderdale, then to Miami and a night flight to Rio. Gary's representative for the Rio outing was Curtis Person of Memphis, Tennessee. He met us at the Rio Airport and took us to our hotel. Later that first day, we met the five other couples who elected to play in Rio. Curtis and his widower friend from Memphis arranged a dinner party in the Copa Cabana section of the city. After dinner, we walked along the beach-front, and were amazed to see how many locals were in the water in the dark. The next day we two took a cab with Curtis and his friend to a hill station where we saw beautiful flower gardens in the foothills west of the city. We then flew across the South Atlantic, landing in Johannesburg, where we joined the Gary Player golf tour.

In 1988 we boarded the "Sea Cloud" for a whale-watching trip to the Pacific side of Baja California and the Sea of Cortez with Joe, Tom, and their wives. We boarded a plane at Loreto for the trip via Los Angeles to Philadelphia. This was the winter that the Bucklin company of Northeast Harbor had started the renovation of Carol's 1895 house, the plans having been drawn up by her daughter, Sandra. We were there in March and part of April where we celebrated my 72nd birthday. On the way home we drove through Deerfield and visited art galleries. Carol was pleased with the progress of the Bucklin carpenters but the work was not yet fully completed.

In 1987, having sold my house in Portola Valley, I had contemplated having a place of my own again, rather than staying at the Stanford faculty club during this period of traveling and contesting an insurance company's decision. I sought an apartment in Sequoias, Portola Valley. A studio was available and I took possession of it on 2 Nov. 1990. This is where I am now as I write this, a brilliant decision! In order to be accepted into the Sequoias, I had to spend 90 days in residence which was completed on Jan 30, 1991.

Carol had a memorial service for her mother at St. Davids Church Radnor PA in early January. Mrs. Hollingsworth had been 101 when she died 31 Dec 1990. This was Carol's 70th birthday year and she invited all 5 grandchildren and both sons-in-law to be her guests at Zermatt in Switzerland. I was the photographer. There was plenty of skiing and hiking in this beautiful area. We returned to Philadelphia in early April.

Galapagos trip

In 1992 I invited my four sons and two daughters-in-law to join Carol and me on a trip with a group including the Masters to visit Ecuador and the Galapagos. Our good luck was the snorkeling off the islands, but unfortunately Mark did not get his passport in time to be with us.

In 1993 a trip to Costa Rica was planned by our travel agent friends, the Fieldings of Villanova. We were joined by a group from the Beaumont and went first to the Atlantic side. Our group included Cynthia and Joe, Wendy and Tom. While there, we toured the coastal areas, did a lot of bird watching, and had a fun time white-water rafting down the Reventzon river. Then there was a long bus ride to Monta Verde where we visited the cloud forest, and from there we took a boat ride to a beach on an island in the Pacific. In May of 1993 we made the decision to apply for a Villa at Beaumont. The summer was spent at Northeast Harbor.

Carol invited her two daughters and five grandchildren to be her guests for a week of pony trekking on the Connemara trail in County Galway around Easter of 1995. Carol had done this before with the Irish rider, Willie Leahy. She suggested I invite my daughter, Cynthia and granddaughter, Erin to come with my son,

Joe, and grandson, Alex. This we did, and the highlight for Alex was viewing the monument in the peat bog near Clifden. This was where Alcock and Brown crash landed after their successful transatlantic flight in June 1919.

In June Frank and Margaret Goodyear invited us to be their guests at his ranch in Cody. I arranged that we would visit my son Mark in Meeker before flying from Denver to Cody. The weather was great and Mark showed us the spring beauty of the western slopes.

In February of 1996 we had the opportunity to take a trip to the Seychelles in the Indian Ocean as well as a visit to East Africa. While we were in Kenya there was an opportunity to fly to Lake Victoria and take a trip on a fishing boat. We chose to do this and the sights as we flew were wondrous. Our boat guide was most helpful; we were wearing our swim suits, and after Carol caught a large fish, we both had a dip in the lake. We took a different route on our flight back to our camp. The next day we flew to the Seychelles, where we boarded an Italian-crewed boat and visited several islands in the chain. In April we were fortunate to have the Whelans as our guests at the Merion Golf Club as a celebration of my 80th birthday.

The Swarthmore College Alumni Association sponsored a trip in April 1997 featuring the showplaces of the Hudson Valley Historical Society. We drove there, visiting for the second time, the hometown of my father in Cold Spring. We then drove to the hotel in White Plains area which was our headquarters as we visited different houses each morning and afternoon for four days. This was a pleasant tour with many "old" Swarthmore friends in the group.

Carol joined me in meeting my 1937 classmates for my 60th Reunion on the Swarthmore campus in June. Although I usually joined the golf outing at the nearby golf club in prior years, I decided not to do that so Carol might be able to visit some newer classmates at the luncheon on the campus in the new Kohlberg building. What was most pleasant was that Nancy and Jim Buckingham came from New York and we sat together at lunch.

We were looking forward to January 1999, having booked our fourth trip on the Sea Cloud for a garden trip beginning in the Barbados. This was to be lead by Patrick Bowes, an Irish Expert, and was attended by many members of the NYC chapter of the Garden Club of America. This was a great trip but I was concerned about whether I should have one knee replaced. Carol agreed to go to California with me in February and we visited Stockton and Jinkie Rush in San Francisco. Carol stayed several days with them while I moved on to the Sequoias. My primary physician suggested a consultation with an Orthopedist at the Palo Alto Medical Foundation. I saw Dr. Lannin the next day at the clinic. He agreed that I was a good candidate and suggested that the right knee should be done first. He had an opening in his operating schedule in August. I let him know that I was still living in Philadelphia and would continue under the care of Dr. Good rather than having the surgery at that time. Back in Villanova, I saw Dr. Good again and he gave me an operating date and on May 26 the joint was replaced at Bryn Mawr Hospital with subsequent rehab at Paoli.

On the Sea Cloud

As the new century began, the problems with Carol's 870 Lesley Road house maintenance continued. She said yes to every villa and apartment she was shown at the Beaumont except two, one of which had a swimming pool in the lower level, and the other a movie theater. My other knee was bothersome but, with time, I seemed to have less trouble with the left knee and the right was much better after the replacement. We accepted every invitation to travel in the bad weather joining friends to go cross country skiing in Squaw Valley with Jane Langhorne and skiing with the Purdys at Squaw Valley in January. In February we went to the Antarctic with a Salen Lindblad group. In April I asked Erin and her mother, Cynthia, to join Carol and me in Reunion 2000 in late April in Kunming, the eastern base the hump fliers used to empty their cargo.

At Christmas we visited the Purdys, and, while there, we agreed to join them in a family outing on a boat owned by an Eskimo tribe that wintered in the Sea of Cortez in Mexico. Carol and I flew from Philadelphia to Phoenix and then to Loreto, and met the Purdys there. This was a fun time except when I had to sit in the kayaks with my stiff knees. Carol and I flew back to Phoenix and spent the weekend at the Arizona Biltmore. After the long weekend we returned to Villanova. On the 9ᵗʰ of March, we flew to Jacksonville and had lunch at Amelia Island before we boarded the Clipper ship for a voyage north with a group of retired physicians enjoying the sights of the inland waterway north to Charleston. There we stayed at the B & B recommended by Cynthia Drayton and visited the current Drayton plantation before flying back north to Philadelphia. After spring and autumn in Philadelphia and summer in Northeast Harbor, we spent Christmas week in Sanibel, Florida with Grandfather John Purdy and his family.

The first three months of 2002 were wintry and depressing. What helped was to interact with my oldest grandson, Alex, who was in his first year at the Phelps School in Malvern, Pa. When he arrived in September he was in summer clothes. As the weather got colder I would bring him winter clothes that I was no longer using. The result was that we had many pleasant visits together; a rare opportunity for a grandfather. Carol's only grandson, William Rush Purdy, had taken a job in San Francisco with Enterprise Rental Car. Carol wanted to visit him in San Francisco so we flew there from Philadelphia on April 9ᵗʰ. We were able to be with Will on his time off and the opportunity came for Will to meet all of my family when my eldest Granddaughter, Erin was playing on the Cal women's lacrosse team in a game against Stanford in Palo Alto. It was great fun with Alex leading cheers for the Cal girls but Stanford scored in the final minute to win the game.

In June the weather warmed, the sun dried out the Northeast Harbor course, and I was able to get around using the Buick Skylark that we garaged there over the winter. Carol arrived in mid June She was happy to be in the modernized 1895 house which her daughters had insisted on renovating with modern appliances in the bathroom and kitchen. I kept busy when not on the golf course by getting rid of the clutter in the basement and picking up the fallen branches in the side yard which the local gardeners hauled away. Mark told Wendy and Tom that he had arranged for a friend to take care of his animals for Christmas week and that he was anxious to spend Christmas with them. I told Carol that I appreciated Molly's invitation to be in Durham with the Purdys again but that I was going to Portola Valley to be with Mark and Wendy and Tom's family. I stayed at 11H during my visit and returned to Villanova in early January 2003.

Back in Villanova, Carol told me she had friends in the local garden club who were talking about a trip with Patrick R. Bowe beginning in Antigua and ending in Barbados. The trip was to be in the new sailing ship, Sea Cloud II. Patrick Bowe, after a heart bypass was great, and we arranged to stay extra days at the Colony hotel at the beach at Barbados. By early February we were back at 870 Lesley Road. In the spring we were involved in a family get-together for Jessica's graduation from Brown and Anne's graduation from St. Pauls. When we arrived back at 870 Lesley Road, Carol was notified by Beaumont that a villa at 66 Middle Road would be available for her inspection on Thanksgiving weekend. Carol and I liked the two floors and it was just what Carol wanted. She arranged to have some painting and carpeting and we moved in on Feb. 3, 2004.

My eldest granddaughter, Erin was at Berkeley in her fourth year playing on the women's lacrosse team. I went to California for some of the home games in February and March and then back to 66 Middle. Erin's graduation was in May and I flew to Sacramento to be with Cynthia and Joe, and we drove to the campus and met Tom and Wendy for Erin's graduation in mid May.

Jessica was to be married to David Axelrod in August 2005 at Lakeside, MI. Mollie wanted another car there, so she came and drove Carol's Subaru to Michigan. We went to Maine in late June 2004 in Carol's Toyota Prius making the 600 mile trip in 10 hours with only one stop (not for gas) getting 55 miles per gallon. In March 2004 when I paid my annual dues, I decided to resign from Merion where I had belonged since 1958. This was primarily because my golf and bridge-playing member friends were either dying or unable to play. While I had been approved by Beaumont's administration to live with Carol at 66 Middle paying the couple rate, I was not part of their medical care program. Having the Sequoias lifecare plan, I worked out a separation agreement and left Carol on 29ᵗʰ Dec. 2005.

While recuperating from my May 1999 complete right knee replacement, I had the opportunity to request senior status at San Francisco Golf Club. This was granted in 2000 by the Board of Directors. With my change of residence in the Philadelphia area in late 2005 to the Sequoias in Portola Valley, I was fortunate enough to host a luncheon on April 2, 2006 to celebrate my 90ᵗʰ birthday with family and fellow Sequoia golfers. Easter brunch in 2006 with Gary Harmon and the Kruegers was most enjoyable as well as the 2007 Easter buffet with my family.

Part II
What The Game Of Golf Has Meant To Me: 1926 To 2007

1. Golfing in the Twenties

My father and mother lived on the north side of Youngstown on Lexington Avenue. Across the street was the north boundary of what was left of the Stambaugh family farm. This field was a makeshift baseball play area into which my younger brother, age 5, and I, age 7, intruded by climbing over a fence. Other older boys played baseball but we were too young to join. I was aware that my father bowled, but I was not familiar with anything else he did except to help my mother with gardening. My father had no relatives that I knew about at the time. My mother's closest relative, other than her father, was a younger brother, Frank. He lived on the south side of Youngstown and was a plumber by trade. I knew him to be big and strong. He had been a physical fitness instructor in the Army and was still in the United States when the war ended. He returned to Youngstown to resume his trade as a plumber. He had come by our house when he said he was on his way north to play golf with friends, wearing knickers and a golf shirt.

I was reading the newspaper and familiar with the auto ads and the sports pages. I was aware of an amateur golfer named Bob Jones. He was playing with the pros and beating them in some tournaments. When my uncle told my mother, he was playing with the pros and sometimes winning some of his bets with them, he aroused my curiosity about the game of golf. There was a newspaper reporter named Grantland Rice, who had written up the play of Bob Jones. I read that he had been born in Atlanta in 1902 and that his father played the game and belonged to a club that employed a Scotsman as their professional. Jones, as a boy, took up the game and was skilled enough at age 14 to play in the National Amateur in 1916 when the tournament was held on a course that was then called Merion Cricket "East Course".

Jones did well enough in his first national appearance but was put out in the third round of match play by the defending champion, Robert Gardner of Chicago. He played each season in national competitions and, in 1925, he won the British Open at St. Anne's in England. The next year he played in St. Andrews winning the Open there, with a record-breaking score for 72 holes of 291. This would be "three over even fours". In the later 20s, he had played well at the difficult course in nearby Pittsburgh, the Oakmont Golf Club, and aroused much local interest.

As a 12 year old Boy Scout I was aware that my scoutmaster played the game, and many older men and some women were beginning to play the game. It was early in the spring of 1926 when managers in the steel industry in Youngstown announced the formation of an industrial golf league. My father at the time was 44 and working at the General Fireproofing Company plant. This was just north of the Youngstown North Side city limits. Although he had been an employee of the company from the late 1890s, he was not then a department head or a foreman. However, he was invited to try out for the team by one of his bowling team members even though he informed them he had never played the game. These men, I later learned, were Tom McLaughlin and Paul Arons.

It was announced that the matches would be held at the Doughton Golf course in nearby Hubbard. This was a course laid out in the family's apple orchard by their oldest son, Steve, who was also the course professional. As it turned out, any employee who showed up at the first tee and played was on the team. The lowest foursome gross score was the winner of the day's match. Every swing counted, even though the ball might not have been touched.

My father liked his brother in law, J. Frank Conroy and knew he was keen on golf. He asked Frank to help him get started. Frank encouraged him to give it a try and I joined them in what was my father's first lesson at a practice fairway on the Gypsy Lane Municipal course of the Youngstown Playground Department. This was near our home at 225 Curry Place. This first outing did not discourage my father and he agreed with Frank's offer to help him get clubs and golf togs and to play on the League's opening day at the Doughton course.

Frank and Dad met with his friend, a Frankie Long, who helped him select clubs and a bag. My father also took a beginner's lesson. Years later Frankie Long would welcome me at this Youngstown Muny course as an apprentice caddy. From time to time during the summer and autumn Uncle Frank would call and arrange a time to play with my father and give him tips. I was invited to join, and, keeping up with the sports pages, I had an interest in learning the history of the game and how I might learn to play better with the old clubs Frank gave me.

2. The Caddying Years: 1930 and Later

My first year in Rayen High School began in September, 1929. This was a year of adjustment and I did well in everything except English. Miss Maguire rated me as B, my only grade below A that I received in High School. My 14th birthday was on 2nd April 1930 and I then became eligible to caddy at Youngstown Muny on Gypsy Lane. This was a 10 to 15 minute walk from 225 Curry Place where we were then living. My mother and father encouraged me to try caddying soon after I "became of age". I went to the Muny nearly every week day.

Knowing the professional and caddy master, Frankie Long, I introduced myself and told him I wanted to learn to caddy and earn some money. He then introduced me to a younger man, in golfing attire, who was an assistant pro. This man gave me a short quiz as to what and when I should do to help the golfer to whom I was assigned. I did not get assigned for several visits, but, by mid-May, I was getting a nine hole round twice weekly and being paid 50c a round. It became obvious that at that time of day, 3:30 – 4 pm, I was one of the few caddies available. Together with rounds on weekends with my uncle Frank and father, as well as caddying for my father in the Fireproofing team matches, I was learning golf etiquette "on the job". Usually, on non-match week days, I was done caddying and back home about the time that my parents returned home.

My uncle Frank gave me tips that added to my expertise and this gave me greater self confidence when I was assigned to assist more talented golfers than those who were in the industrial league. I learned that the good caddy, beginning on the first tee, should know when to be quiet and where he should stand before the player took his stance and started his swing. He should watch the ball of each player and where those balls came to rest, using some obvious marker to gauge the distance. Enjoyment is diminished, if one has to hunt for balls. The usual position, before the player addresses the ball, is to place the bag containing all the clubs (13 total) on the ground behind the player within an easy reach for him to select his club. The experienced player knows the distance to the flag, and which club to use for the particular shot. The player should also know when it is his turn to hit; i.e., when his ball is farthest from the flag. It is bad for a member of the foursome to be ahead of the player whose ball is the one to be played. When the player has selected the club, the caddy picks up the bag and steps behind the player so he can watch the flight of the ball. What happens after the first "away" player makes his shot is crucial to the enjoyment of the game. Experienced players know who is next to shoot and have their club ready when it is their turn. Players who are talking, taking several practice swings, and flubbing their shots create confusion and lead to impatience and boredom. A good caddy should never be ahead of the player about to make his shot. He is always silent as he watches the inexperienced, incompetent members of his foursome, including "his man".

In recent years, I have noted that the attendance at club "men's day" outings falls off when there are a large number of older players who have never learned golf etiquette or improved their game so they can play quickly. Those players who are steady, and do play quickly prefer to play at a different time and select their own foursome members. The inadequate golfers consider these fellow members at their club "snobbish".

In the period from 1926 to September 1930, I knew little about the history of golf. When Bob Jones won the U.S. Amateur at Merion Golf Club in Ardmore, PA, the sports world took note that this title was the fourth "major" he had won in 1930. This was referred to as "the grand slam" – a term used not only in baseball, but in auction bridge as well. This was the key to my unlocking the vault containing golf history. A good part of golf history relates to where great championships, both medal and match play, have been held.

In the early 1930's, I knew about the existence of private clubs in the northern part of Youngstown suburbs such as the Youngstown Country and the Squaw Creek Clubs. On this side of town were public clubs such as the Youngstown Muny, on Gypsy Lane, owned by the city and the Doughton course, at nearby suburb Hubbard owned by the family of that name. On the southern side were the Tippecanoe and the Poland Country – private clubs. Also on the southern side was the Mill Creek Park – a public enterprise owned by and operated by a commission of public spirited citizens. Plans were underway to construct public courses on which play required payment of higher greens fees. One of the most prominent food merchants of the city, George Fordyce was a golfer of high profile What was public knowledge was that his family spent time in the autumn and spring at a golfing resort in Southern Pines, NC. This is where the, now famous, Pinehurst Resort is. Courses I knew about then were in Akron, Cleveland, Toledo, and Columbus in Ohio; Oakmont in Pittsburgh; Hershey near Harrisburg; in Philadelphia, the Merion Cricket and Philadelphia Country Club; and in nearby New Jersey, Pine Valley and Baltusrol. In Northeastern PA, Pocono Mountain Area, at Shawnee on the Delaware, Fred Waring, prominent orchestra leader, built a resort to add to Buck Hill competition with the Inn's three 9 hole courses that this Quaker resort provided.

R.T. Jones had won some of his major U.S. titles at some of these already mentioned, Amateur and Open competitions. However, his "Grand Slam" in 1930 made me aware that a club at St. Andrews in Fife, Scotland, The Royal and Ancient, had been sponsoring the British Amateur and Open in England and Scotland since the 1860's. Some that I later had the chance to visit and play in Scotland were: St. Andrews, Carnoustie, Prestwick, Troon, Turnberry, Muirfield and North Berwick. The United States Golf Association was formed in the 1880's by members of some of the earliest private clubs. They sponsored the U.S. Amateur and the U.S. Open. In 1916 the professionals organized the P.G.A. in New York with the financial support of the Philadelphian, Rodman Wanamaker. Their P.G.A. tournament, played at different courses in the U.S.A., was match play for the Wanamaker trophy. It is now medal play and is usually held in August. The Master's Tournament, played at the Augusta National Course designed by Bob Jones and Dr. Alistair Mackenzie, is played every April at Augusta and is the first "major" each year. The other majors are the US Open (June) and British Open (July). My good fortune has been to be at Augusta in April, the US Open at Pebble Beach, Merion (1951), The Country Club in

Brookline (1988), Shinnecock, Long Island (1986), the PGA at Pebble Beach in August (1970s) and the Eisenhower (World Amateur) held on East, at Merion in 1961. British Opens that I have attended were St. Andrews (1984) and Turnberry (1986).

One of the most outstanding golf historians I came to know about after 1945 was Bernard Darwin, an Oxford graduate, golfer, and reporter of Champions "between the wars". From that history I learned of American golfers who did well in British events. These were R.T. Jones, Jr., R.A. Gardner of Chicago,

At Spyglass

who was the grandfather of my golf instructor at Northeast Harbor (N.E.H.G.C.), Robert Gardner III. Other American amateurs were Jesse Sweetster, Lawson Little of Stanford, Robert Sweeney, and Charlie Yates. Those who won the Open in addition to R.T. Jones Jr. were: Walter Hagen, Gene Sarazen, Denny Shute, and Tommy Armour. Tommy came to the US after WW I and earned the reputation of being an outstanding writer and teacher of golf. His book, "How to Play Your Best Golf All the Time" has been reprinted as One of the "Classics" of Golf instruction.

At the time Armour's book was first published, he was the teaching pro at the Florida Boca Raton Club. This, in the late 20s, was one of the first golf/spa resorts in the USA. In the forward to "The Classic", Herbert Warren Wind, an outstanding USA Golf historian, notes that the Boca Raton Club was organized and constructed by Clarence Geist of Philadelphia. This Mr. Geist was a patient of my father-in-law, B.A. Thomas, a Philadelphia urologist. Mr. Geist, a grateful patient, made Dr. Thomas an honorary member not only at the Boca Raton Club, but also the Sea View Country Club in Absecon, New Jersey. This venue was on the New Jersey coast close to the causeway to Atlantic City. Geist did for the water supply in Philadelphia what Bourne of Filoli/Killarney fame did for water in the San Francisco Bay area. Golf resorts and spas which I have been able to enjoy are Seaview, Ojai, Pebble Beach, Mauna

Kea, Turnberry and Gleneagles in Scotland, and Banff and Jasper in Canada, as well as Waterville and Ballybunion in Ireland.

3. Playing Opportunities While a Student: 1933 – 1942

During the school year, there was no thought of golf. After classes ended in May 1934, a group in Wolman House decided to borrow clubs and play at a public course in Wallingford just across the Crum Creek on Swarthmore Village's western boundary. Later, I learned that this property was once owned by Lucinda's grandfather: Powell Stackhouse. After his death in 1927 his estate had been sold to Mary Lyon School whose president arranged for a 9 hole course to be laid out for the use of the women. The public could use the course for a minimal greens fee. This is where we played. Jim Buckingham, who had never held a golf club before that outing, had a 45 for 9 holes, the best score for the group, most of who had played before. Jim was a natural athlete and lettered in football, basketball (he was captain in his junior year) and baseball.

When I was in Youngstown for summer vacation, I played at the Youngstown municipal course with Rayen High classmates Regis Gilboy and Dan Gibbon. Later Lutz Flynn joined us along with John Stotler, Jimmy Patrick and John Newman. My cousin, E.T. Butler Jr., stayed with us one summer and we also played together.

I did not bring my clubs to 1013 N. Broadway during my first year at Johns Hopkins. The summer after my first year I spent in Northern Arizona. While in Flagstaff, as a guest of Ed Jakel, a good golfer, I played with him on a course near the San Francisco Mountain, north of the town. The course had sand greens. I played well enough with borrowed clubs that I decided to take the several clubs I had collected to Baltimore for my next three years in medical school. The nearest course to my lodging, at Miss Susie Slagles' at 1013 N. Broadway was in Clifton Park. This was then a Baltimore City Municipal Park. In the 1850's it had been the estate of the Quaker merchant Johns Hopkins. His will instructed his executors to found the University, a hospital, and a medical school. Several physicians who took their meals at 1013 were aspiring golfers. Those who invited me to join them at Clifton were Robert

Wilkins, Calvin Kay and A.M. Harvey. Harvey later was the Osler professor at Hopkins. After he retired he came to California with his wife, who was a year behind me as a medical student. We played together at San Francisco Golf Club and also at Pasatiempo near Santa Cruz. This course was designed by the Scottish physician Alistair Mackenzie, who had also designed Cypress Point at Pebble Beach.

When I graduated from medical school, my mother gave me a set of matched clubs and a bag that she had seen on sale at the leading hardware store in downtown Youngstown. These clubs I used when I played in the USA from 1941 to 1958 when I was elected as a member in Merion. in 1958. The one occasion I had to play while an intern was the invitation from the medical resident Dr. John Sayen. He was my teacher on the medical wards and arranged for me to have an afternoon off on a beautiful July day to be driven by him in his roadster, top down, to a public course in Valley Forge.

In Sept. 1942 we went to Kentucky and from there to San Antonio, Texas. My first duty station as an aviation physiologist was at Peyote, Texas. We were there from Christmas, 1942 until the early summer of 1943.

In late September, I left Lucinda in Miami and joined a group of officers going to India by way of Brazil and West Africa. Because my work was scheduled to be at a "hump-flying training school", which had not yet activated, I was assigned to various bases. At one base, I was offered the opportunity to join a group who were going to be flown, first to New Delhi, and then to western India for a short trip from there to Srinagar, Kashmir. After a day or so there, I learned that several officers had decided to go further up the hills in Kashmir to a resort area said to be at 10,000 ft elevation. We were driven in a truck for several hours and reached an impassable road. We were told that we had to walk the remaining half mile to the guest house. The next day at breakfast, I met a group who planned to go to the golf course and then have a picnic lunch. That is how I was able to play golf in Kashmir.

4. Family, Career and Residence Changes

After my service discharge, Dec 1945, there was not only the return to Lucinda, but also the opportunity to teach and study in the Pharmacology Dept of Penn on a Rockefeller Foundation fellowship. Living in the apartment was not an option and we purchased a lot and contracted with a builder to erect a two story house at 1458 Hampstead Road in Penn Wynne. . Sometime in that first year my Swarthmore pre-med classmate, Dr. Ward Fowler and his wife, Joan, moved near us in Penn Wynne. They told us about the golf course on Earlington Road in Penn Wynne. I started playing there with Ward and Joan Kelley Fowler. After Tom arrived on 1st August 1947, I arranged for a semester course in medical instrumentation in the Biology department of the graduate school at M.I.T.

In May 1952 we moved from Penn Wynne to Merion. Soon after we settled, I was invited to join the American Legion, post #545. This group of veterans met in the Merion War Tribute House on Hazlehurst Avenue. I began to play golf in the spring-summer months with this group. Their outings were held at private clubs hosted by the Legion member who was a member of that club.

In our first year at Merion, we met the Whelan family, then living on Baird Road. He invited me to be his guest at Aronimink. Soon after playing there, he urged me to join Philadelphia Doctors Golf. This group held outings much like the Post. Over the period of four to five years I had playing experience at about six or seven private clubs. I had known about Merion since 1930 and it became my first choice. Playing with Merion post #545 golfers and trying to participate each year in the Merion Golf Club outing, I met Bob Barker, a member of Merion, who often hosted the group. I knew my choice and let Bob know how much I enjoyed playing at Merion. In 1957 I asked him about joining. He was most helpful and made me aware of the physician members who might be my sponsors. With the help of Dr. Flippin, David Cooper and the Swarthmore alumnus, who was then chairman of the admissions committee, Lucinda and I were invited to join in 1958. The same year, I was

Board Certified in Internal Medicine so I did not consider the club membership a luxury but more a reward for "arriving".

With Steve Whelan at Merion

I was not a member of Merion Golf Club very long when I was asked to drive to Pittsburgh with Dr. Joe Wagner, a cardiologist at Bryn Mawr Hospital. He was a member of Philadelphia Country Club and was attending the Annual Pennsylvania Medical Assn. Meeting in Pittsburgh in order to join the Association's golf outing at the world famous club, Oakmont. After enjoying the golf experience, during cocktail hour, I was asked to host the golf outing at Merion Golf Club at the meeting the next year in Philadelphia. This I did with the help of drug company representatives who provided everybody with tee prizes and suitable awards for low gross and low net scorers. This was fun for me and many members told me how much they had enjoyed it. There were several physician Merion members of the Philadelphia Doctors Golf Association. Each year the first outing was at Pine Valley. I did have as guests of mine at Merion, Judge Jim Buckingham, Swarthmore '37, Palmer Futcher, MD one of my Hopkins teachers, John Sayen, MD, who took me golfing when I was an intern, Dr. Jack Hopkins, a fellow Lankenau staff member and many times, Dr. Steve Whelan, my dermatologist and neighbor; as well as Lucinda's cousin, Powell Stackhouse MacCalla.

Our friends, Virginia and Steve Whelan entertained us at their home, 401 Baird, Aronimink Golf Club, and were our hosts at their Seaview Country Club in Absecon, N.J. Lucinda was aware of Mr. Geist's gift to her father but she had never been to the club. She enjoyed the invitation to go there for weekends, but only occasionally played "the Bay Course". While our 19th St. house was being built, we frequently would be weekend guests of the Whelan's at Seaview, playing golf early on Saturdays, and driving up to Long Beach Island to monitor completion of construction. It was at this time, after much discussion, that we decided that a membership at Seaview was "part of the package".

5. Looking Back On Membership at Merion: 1958 – 2005

This opportunity, viewed now in my 91st year, has been the center piece of my golfing experience. My introduction to the professional then, Fred Austin, son-in-law of the great English golf teacher, Ernest Jones, equipped me with an understanding of how a top golf club should be lead.

Fred was a great teacher with particular interest for beginning boys and girls and the play of the women's team in the Annual Philadelphia Golf Association Spring Competition. Interestingly, I never saw him playing the course. What was special for new members was his urging play at open times (7:45 – 8:15) on Saturdays and Sunday in the golf season (April thru Sept.) After Fred retired, he was followed by Bill Kittelman. Bill continued Fred's leadership and was particularly responsible for the superior showing of the women's team play in the Philadelphia Golf Association, spring team competitions. Hugh Wilson, a member, designed not only the East Course where the many USGA championships were conducted, but also an 18 hole West Course. This was where we played as a family on weekends, all of our sons having been enrolled in Fred Austin's junior golf teaching sessions each spring. In the period 1958 to 1965 I played on Wednesday afternoons with Dr. Malcolm Miller, who was the senior MD in S. 302 Lakenau Medical Bldg. We were joined by Malcolm's longtime friend, John Y Mace, Esq., later my lawyer. We usually played behind the foursome of J. Howard Pew, of Sun Oil, who made it possible for the golf club in WWII years to split from the Merion Cricket Club – 1945.

One Saturday in 1961–1962, I arrived at the first tee of the East course at 07:15. The starter matched me with two members, older than I, whom I did not know. After the round, which was most pleasant, we had lunch together. We were about to leave, when one of the men said, "Doctor, perhaps you should think of updating your golf clubs". He went on to say, "You seem to be established in your profession and a member of this great club, but you are playing with 1929–1933 made (mass produced) clubs. You will play better with 1960 models." I thanked him and later learned he and his partner were Sears-Roebuck executives whose company had mass produced these clubs in the 30's. These were the set my mother presented to me in 1941. Soon after I asked Fred Austin about new clubs and he suggested I consult the previous Merion professional, George Sayer, who had a golf club shop in Haverford. I went there and was fitted by George and his son. Later I learned he was a descendant of a Scottish club maker, who had made a putter which I had bought from our professional, Robert Gardner in Northeast Harbor, Maine in the 1980's. By obtaining an antique golf club catalogue, I was able to learn that it had been produced in the 1890s. This showed the mark that several generations of Sayers Scottish club makers had put on the clubs that were manufactured in their shops. Gardner was helpful in convincing me that this putter was old. Also, he said he thought it would be more valuable if the shaft and grip were worked on by an antique club specialist. I accepted his suggestion and was pleased with the result.

Sometime in the 1990's, playing at Sunnybrook Golf Club, I was in a golf clinic conducted by professional John Allen. Noting my slice with metal woods, he suggested an offset shaft made by Cobra. He loaned me a set for several weeks. I used these clubs and realized they increased my accuracy. He gave me a good buy on a new Cobra set and that is what I use now with a "hog" putter. I also use a sand wedge as a pitching iron that I bought in 1966 from the Palo Alto Municipal Pro, Pat Maloney, which I found in the "one dollar bargain barrel." Knowing I was going to resign from Merion in March 2005 and having a liking for the new Merion Pro, Scott Nye I gave him the 1960 set and the 1890 putter, hoping he would have them displayed on a rack in the Merion Golf Club Shop. In the May/June issue of the publication "Links" is a story by the Philadelphia golfer/historian, James W. Finegan. This is the best short history of the Merion Golf Club that I have read.

6. 1965: The Move to San Francisco

We decided in January 1965 to accept the Sandoz Basel offer to be the medical director of their west coast office. The realtors of Cornish and Carey helped us to buy the 415 Palm Street House. One of their associates helped me to get homeowner's policy coverage. During those meetings he learned that I had elected for non-resident status at Merion Golf and Seaview Country Club. He asked if I, working at 450 Sutter, had any interest in the Olympic Club nearby. Responding positively, he agreed to set in motion the process of sponsorship for membership in the City Club, as well as golfing play on the two 18 hole courses west of Lake Merced. Some time in October, I was told that my membership was approved and I completed my enrollment. Most days I rode the train, but on Fridays I started to drive one of our two cars to the city and parked it in the convenient 450 Sutter garage. After my 4:30 pm office closing, (I was at the office at 7:30-8:00 am), I would drive out to the golf courses on the "great highway." I was surprised on those Fridays to see how few members were on the "Lake Course" at that time. I would play 9 holes in less than 2 hours and then drive 35 miles to Palo Alto. On most of those Fridays I observed a blond teenager who was frequenting the pro shop/caddy shack area who I later learned was the young Johnny Miller. The U.S. Open was scheduled for the Lake Course in June 1966. Johnny posted the low amateur score. Later, I learned that in 1965-66 he was being tutored by the teaching pro at SFGC, and that his parents had obtained a junior membership at Olympic Club, where he played. Ten years later when he won the British Open, he displayed his trophies at SFGC.

In 1966, I learned that a Merion golf member, Bud Greene, was then in San Francisco supervising the advertising office of N.W. Ayer. He was chairman of a Philadelphia MIT fund raising committee on which I served briefly in 1951-52. I phoned Greene and welcomed him to town, although I had never seen or played golf with him at Merion. We had lunch soon after and he said he wanted me to meet his wife. In a few weeks we had hosted them at a dance party at the Olympic Golf clubhouse. Our wives liked each other, particularly when they learned we played bridge as well as golf.

I continued using the Olympic Club golf courses after I joined the Palo Alto Medical Clinic, working at the new Cowell Student Health Center on the Stanford campus. The acting medical chief then was Jim McClenahan, MD. Jim periodically invited each MD into his office to inquire how things were going and whether there was anything he might do for me. Two aspirations came to mind: 1) is it possible for me to work in the Stanford Hospital cardiac clinic part of one afternoon each week, and 2) how to get into Stanford golf?

I said that I had heard that there was the possibility for Stanford full-time staff to be members of the Stanford Golf Club by obtaining the approval of President Sterling. He said he would explore both requests. While working at Stanford Student Health, 1967 – 1969, socially we were meeting friends of Mary Will and Brydon Greene. Many were members of SFGC and we often played there. By 1968, I was playing at Stanford on weekends and inviting friends such as Joe Whitley and Bud Greene to join me. Later, when I went into private practice at 1101 Welch Road, Medical Plaza Palo Alto, I played on Wednesday mornings with Palo Alto MDs such as Pat Gray, Carl Bjorn and Stanford surgeons: Norm Shumway and Jim Marks. Other physicians I played with were: Harold Brumm, Homer Hunt and George Laird. I played with J.D. Ball and we won the President's Cup competition. Our net score for 36 holes was 127. Other friends who played in the President's Cup that year (1977) were: Dr. Pat Gray, my urologist, our neighbor on Palm St., Dr. John Lewis and my friend at the Sequoias, John Donegan. Dr. and Mrs. Harold Brumm played with us in the 50th Anniversary Celebration Tournament in1980, and our team won a silver plate. On the days when the Stanford women's golf team had home matches, I would follow them in the late afternoon.

While I was working in the student health clinic, Tom Watson, Stanford '72, came in with a skin rash. I learned that he had been in parts of the Stanford course, dense with poison oak bushes. He was not aware of the danger of poison oak or ivy as a skin irritant. He was treated with Cortisone cream and healed quickly.

Later I followed him in matches at Shinnecock, Pebble Beach, St. Andrews, and Turnberry. He sent me an autographed picture in 1960's. I never had a chance to watch the Stanford Men's golf team at their matches but I did follow the women's team. That is how I met Sally Voss (now Dr. Krueger, an anesthesiologist in San Francisco) and a member of SFGC. Also I met Julie Inkster there when she was playing with the San Jose State women's team. She told me she grew up on Pasatiempo near Santa Cruz.

In 1969 I had the opportunity of resuming private practice at 1101 Welch Road. It was then that we accepted the invitation of the Greene's and Madden's to share a house at Carmel for the Bing Crosby Pro Am Tournament. At this time Bud Greene said, "I am proposing you for a membership in SFGC, and Helen Madden, chairman of a women's committee at SFGC, is proposing Lucinda for membership in the women's annex." Concurrently Lucinda had become a member of the Women's SF Town and Country Club, sponsored by the wife of Harry Baker, a member of SFGC and Patty Standish Jacobson, whose husband David was one of Stanford's president Wallace Sterling's inner circle. Lucinda liked the SF contacts and joined in 1977. This was possible because of the energy and enthusiasm of Brydon Greene and his people skills to positively affect the outcome of his efforts. He was on the admission committee from 1976 to 1977.

Lucinda was playing at SGFC with Helen Madden and Mrs. Bob Mackenzie on Tuesdays and Thursdays. My golf was limited to Saturday mornings and, occasionally with Lucinda, on Sundays. Dobson Kilduff, a bridge and golf player was our financial advisor. He had a house in Carmel and shared that with his ex wife. He belonged to Cypress Point and he hosted the Maddens, Joe and Cynthia and me to play at Cypress in 1983 and later.

In 1977, Lucinda and I decided to use my membership in the Royal Society of Medicine to stay in their London hotel "Domus Medicus" for a starting place in a U.K. "Roots" trip in May 1977. Lucinda's father, B.A. Thomas, M.D., had researched the Welch ancestors of his family and was aware of a Buchanan castle near Glasgow that had a golf course on the estate which we planned to visit.

Soon after my father died in August 1971, we went to Oahu in the Hawaiian Islands to attend a medical meeting and see the beach life. Gary Garrison told us where to stay and what to do. On this trip we did not take our golf clubs. But we did stay next to the US Officers Club and looked over the nearby golf courses and went to Luau in the evenings. We returned to Portola Valley, having moved there in 1968, and resolved to explore some of the other islands and to take our golf clubs on future trips. In 1972, we took an alumni abroad trip to Japan, Hong Kong, Bangkok. I went to Rangoon, then to Indonesia. Lucinda went shopping in Jog Jakarta and I played golf on the island of Bali.

My chief, in 1978, had approved a three week leave for a trip to attend the Australia Medical Association Cancer Meeting in Adelaide in November. This was another "alumni flights abroad" trip to New Zealand, Australia, Barrier Reef, Tasmania, Melbourne, Ayers Rock and a stop in Fiji on return trip back to the US. We did not bring golf clubs but we did have lunch on the porch of Royal Sydney Golf Club with Lady Mackay and her daughter. I had met them in Simla and stayed with them in New Delhi in 1945. My only golf was with rented clubs and an Indian caddy on Fiji. The caddy was great and I remember the course as being very dry and my shots getting a great roll, but unfortunately they were not very accurate.

In 1981, my financial advisor was Jane Williams, who was helping us with Lucinda's trust funds. Jane's mother, Mary Sewall, whom I had known from the 1940 summer at Small Point, Maine, came to Portola Valley with Jane's father, Lewis Hyde. We entertained them and heard from them about a trip they were planning to join with destinations: Pakistan, Kashmir, Nepal, New Delhi, Agra, the Taj Mahal and Jaipur. Lucinda said, "Let's see if we might join." This was possible and so we departed, meeting the Hydes in the East for the flight to Karachi. Although we did not pack golf clubs, in Kashmir we decided to join a smaller selection of the group going in the hills above Srinagar. I had played golf in Gulmarg in 1944 and I was able to get 8 of the group to sign for this side trip. This was one of the most fun days on the trip.

7. Testing Resiliency: 1983-1984

After Lucinda's Death, I concentrated on my work at the extended care division of the VA Hospital Menlo Park campus. There was a 3 hole par 3 length course, which I used each weekday on my lunch hour. The greens were fast and this was great practice for my short game and putting. On Saturdays, I drove the 37 miles up to San Francisco Golf Club (SFGC) and had my breakfast there. I usually was with the widower Larry Hamilton, and we would join the other members who had finished breakfast when we did. One Saturday, a new member, George Schultz, appeared just as we were finishing and asked if anybody was ready to join him. We did, and that was one of the few times I ran around the course in order to keep up with George. It was not golf as I knew, the enjoyable kind. Sundays I did the same, usually after early mass and breakfast at home. I usually played with Stan Madden, Harry Baker, Sam Stewart, George Cronin, John Dean and occasionally with Henry Clausen and Bruce Swartz. I had proposed Gary Harmon for membership and he was elected 18 May 1982. Occasionally he played with me, but his game was in the low 80's and he soon found younger members who also played well.

Although, I joined SFGC in July 1977, I was still a member of Stanford Golf Club. Lucinda had enjoyed playing there with the women, several of whom were Doctor's wives. She did not play after May 1982, and although I played mostly elsewhere, I was reluctant to resign. Dr. George Wilson and his wife played there. On at least one occasion, I joined them. Dr. Wilson was my Dermatologist, having his

With Stan Madden
and Henry Clausen at SFGC

office also at the Medical Plaza, 1100 Welch Road. I was told that the Wilsons had signed up for a trip to Europe in September 1983 to play golf in Portugal and Spain. He suggested I try to join the group. Although I was interested in this, I knew it would be difficult to get leave time in September. However, I asked and, to my surprise, was able to get the time off.

In mid-September we flew from SFO to Lisbon and were bussed to the Algarve to the golf Resort, "Penina". This Resort-Golf course was designed and operated by Henry Cotton, the English professional and world class player. After he retired he was full time at Penina, giving lessons and doing everything possible to attract golfers to the large hotel on the property. This was our HQ while we played there and on several nearby courses to which we were bussed. The summer of 1983 was dry and the courses in that part of the Algarve were "Burnt Out". The greens were fast and there was a good roll, but not much fun. The Wilsons had rented a car so that each afternoon after golf, we motored to the sea ports and went on the piers to see what the fisherman had caught. Then we had dinner at places nearby that the locals recommended. That was most fun and memorable. After the first week we were bussed into Spain and traveled far east on the Costa del Sol. The courses there were too long and difficult for the game I had at the time. We visited several wineries as we worked our way west and, after playing at the beautiful Soto Grande resort, we flew to Madrid and then home.

My boyhood friend, Dan Gibbon, a part time golfer and a full time partner of Covington and Burling attorneys, asked me to join him in a game at Chevy Chase Club. This I did when I traveled there with Joanna. This was a pleasant occasion, as was a time earlier that I played there as a guest of Henry Clausen of SFGC.

Sometime after I returned to Portola Valley, I realized how well organized and reasonably priced the trip to Spain had been. Knowing I was to retire 31 December, I had already signed up for a continuing medical education trip to the Antarctic in January. I decided that the experience of golfing in Europe, particularly the U.K., was something I enjoyed and wanted to do more. The "Wide World of Golf" tour leader had told me about his hopes of finalizing a tour in Scotland that would end in Fife, so we could be at St. Andrews for the July "British Open" intrigued me. I asked to be put on his list and in December, when I heard from him that the tour was on, I signed his contract to be with them in early July.

I was given a world Atlas by my nurses when they had a farewell party around Christmas 1983. I retired 31 Dec.

My golf in February and March was improving with play at San Francisco on Tuesday, Thursday and Saturday. I decided I would try to get to opening day at Merion Golf Club. The weather in April at Merion was splendid and my play there was good enough to make the trip worthwhile. I spent some time with the Whelans, and then visited a widow, Bodine Lamont, at her summer place in Vinyl Haven, driving there with her from her townhouse outside Portland, Maine. When I returned from Maine, I was called by Joanna asking if I would be able to go to Paris and then on to Bergen, Norway to take a North Cape Cruise with her.

My trip to Antarctica was enhanced by one of the naturalists. He later called me and asked me if I had any interest in a Baltic Sea Cruise he was leading using the "Polaris", which was our boat in the Antarctic. I told him that I had planned to join the "Wide World of Golf" group for the British open in Scotland in July. He did not know when the Polaris was to leave Copenhagen and sail through the Baltic Sea, east to Leningrad and return using a different route. It turned out that there was a significant interval after the Norwegian mail boat returned to Bergen, and when the Polaris was to sail from Copenhagen. Joanna suggested that this was a good time to take me to the apartment she had purchased in Sete and to have me play a golf course she knew to be near there. We bought a Eurail pass and used that to get to the south of France. I played the golf course which was nearer Avignon than Sete. Then I left Joanna in Sete and took the train to Copenhagen.

On arrival at the Copenhagen train station, I asked a tourist counter whether there were any B and B's near a Golf course but there were none. In fact there was only one B and B available and that was run by a widower whose house was near a suburban train station. I went there using my Eurail pass and liked the arrangement so well that I stayed there until the Polaris set sail. My host discouraged me from trying to play golf because there were no convenient public courses. He, knowing about the rail pass, encouraged me to visit the islands of the country west of Copenhagen, to which all ferries accepted the pass. I happened to learn about the island that was the home for the recording and printing of the underground resistance to the German occupation in Denmark in WWII. I visited that island several times and bought paperback copies of the five or six volumes that had been published up to that time. Over the time I was abroad, I read all of those books and was so impressed with what had been done that I decided to take them with me back to the USA. Later, still having those books when I became a member of SFGC, I heard Frank Tatum (Sandy) tell a story of how in 1940s while at Oxford as a Rhoads Scholar, he was invited by a Danish friend to visit Denmark for the week that "The Danish Open" was held. His story of how he happened to win the Open was a most amusing tale. So on my next visit to SFGC, I took the books to Sandy's Locker and presented them to him.

On the Polaris, we had a skipper, who was Swedish, and a golfer. He, on the trip eastward to Swedish Islands, found out that there were five or six passengers who had golf clubs with them and at least ten others who played golf, and said they would rent clubs and play at the Swedish course he had in mind. The day came and we had 4 foursomes including the captain. He had arranged a competition. I played well until a lightning storm caused us to flee the course and return to the Polaris. We had played enough to decide, during a special party of drinks, who were the winners. I was one, and I recall my name, date, and score appeared on a plaque in one of the ship's lounges before I left the Polaris. The Captain said he was going to play again on later trips.

It was in early July when we returned to Copenhagen. I took the plane to Glasgow where it had been arranged that I would meet the Carmel California Golf shop Group called "Wide World of Golf". We went from Glasgow to Turnberry and then played Troon and Prestwick. We then went east and played Carnoustie and North Berwick. We were unable to make a connection at Muirfield, chiefly because of the notorious club Secretary, a curmudgeon if there ever was one. We then stayed at Gleneagles and played two of the courses there. We commuted from there to St. Andrews, watching my favorite, Tom Watson, lose a close match on the final day to the Spanish star, Seve Ballesteros. Back in Philadelphia, I stayed with Dr. and Mrs. Whelan. They were receiving my mail and there were several letters for me. There was a letter from there that would change my life for the next 21 years. This was an invitation from Carol Smith Rush to visit her at her house in Northeast Harbor, Maine. Carol and I were married 25 January 1985 in St. Davids Church, Wayne, PA. Both her daughters and two of my sons, Joe and Mark, were there to be with us.

8. Philadelphia Revisited

After our marriage, 25 January, we prepared for our trip to visit the Rodman Pages on Exuma, in the Bahamas. I had told Carol, I wanted to have her join the Gary Player tour of South Africa golfing venues in late February. There was a possible golf outing in Rio, Brazil and we decided to do that after Exuma. At the Pages, we were joined by the Chews and the Starrs. We flew from the Bahamas back to Fort Lauderdale, then to Miami and a night flight to Rio. Gary's representative for the Rio outing was Curtis Person of Memphis, Tennessee. He met us at the Rio Airport and took us to our hotel. Later that first day, we met the five other couples who elected to play in Rio. The golf was in the early morning the next day. All I remember was how hot it was the second nine. We were all very thirsty and a siesta was in order after lunch. Curtis and his widower friend from Memphis arranged a dinner party in the Copa Cabana section of the city. After dinner, we walked along the beach front, and were amazed to see how many locals were in the water in the dark.

We then flew across the South Atlantic landing in Johannesburg. This was the home of Gary's wife, Vivienne Vevey. Her father was one of South Africa's most respected golf teachers. The first day in Johannesburg was at the course where Gary's father-in-law was the teaching professional. Our group was now 12 couples. A clinic was put on by Mr. Vevey, his golf professional son, and Gary Player. After an introduction, we broke up into groups of eight, with each pro giving points of minor change in chip, pitch and putting techniques. Then, in foursomes we played 12 holes, with each professional joining for 4 holes to add personal pointers. After lunch, because of the heat, it was siesta time. That evening we had drinks and dinner at Vivienne and Gary's home. Gary gave a tour of his indoor fitness room, his outdoor putting greens, and a short 3-hole green with sand traps for pitching practice. After dinner, we met some of their six children. Then Gary told of some of his experiences from the year (1958) when he won the British Open.

There was an early morning flight from Joburg East to Durban, a harbor on the Indian Ocean. By the time the 6 foursomes were ready to take the first tee, it was very hot and humid in the bright sun. There was no possibility of a shotgun start, even though Gary might have so planned. The problem was few, if any caddies were present. We did get started eventually, although some foursomes gave up on their caddies because few were sober enough to tote the bags. Gary played 3 holes with each of the 6 foursomes giving tips to each of his guests. He had memorized the names and hometowns of each of his guests and also knew the club or clubs to which they belonged. Curtis Person, who also assisted, was not only a member of a club in Memphis, but also a member of Bobby Jones Masters Club in Augusta. We completed 18 holes, had a light lunch, and were bussed with our clubs and luggage to the airport, where, with Gary and Curtis, we boarded a plane to Cape Town. On the flight South and West, Gary was in the cockpit with the pilot. When we were near his horse ranch, several hundred miles north of Cape Town, Gary came on the mike and pointed out specific parts of his "spread" as the plane circled the area. The other passengers on the plane were surprised and pleased to have this unexpected "show".

Our plane landed in an airport closer to the University town of Stellenbosch, headquarters of the group of people who ran South Africa. This was the location of their church headquarters, their printing presses, Army Headquarters, as well as the Police. We were treated to a vineyard tour, wine tasting and lunch in a beautiful woodsy setting. Gary and his guests were treated splendidly even though Gary's family was from England. I had as a guest fellow in my research unit, 1958-1959 a South African M.D., named Louis Potgieter, an Alumnus of their medical school, and so I had learned a lot about this situation while he was with us. Most of the other 23 golfers were learning about "Apartheid" for the first time. We played a 9-hole course after lunch and then we were bussed to our hotel in Cape Town. The next day we were bussed to a game park where we spent most of the day. The next day, we were driven south to the beach area of South Africa. The final day we played a beautiful 18-hole course; splendid weather with a breeze from the Atlantic. There was a farewell dinner that evening, and we flew to Rio, Miami, and then to Philadelphia, arriving back in Villanova early in the second week in March.

At Merion Golf Club my friend Frank Itgen informed me of his group, most of my age, which came to the club before lunch on Wednesday and Saturdays. Foursomes were formed before lunch and with good weather, we played the East course, teeing off before 12:30 p.m. (Members only). If the weather was not good, we played bridge. We were home only a few days when I received an invitation from Dr. Harold Brumm to stay with the private family, long time friends, in Augusta, Georgia, and have the use of their "Masters Tickets" on Monday, Tuesday and Wednesday. They were to arrive late Wednesday and we were to return their tickets to them Thursday, and share them the remaining three days of the four day tournament. We accepted, and flew to Atlanta and Augusta on Monday of the tournament week. Then in mid April, the weather was beautiful and we had a reunion with Gary Player, who was there to play, and Curtis Person who was a member of the club's hospitality committee. Dr. Brumm and his wife arrived on Wednesday afternoon, and they had a rental car and showed us the sights, having had tickets for the previous 20 years. On Thursday, we rented a car as Carol wanted to visit Aiken; this was a "Horsey" place and a place where one of her friends Winifred Lee D'olier went to boarding school. The school was no longer there but the golf course, on which the school was located, is still there. We walked around that course, went to the outdoor race tracks, noting that most of the jockeys were young women. We visited the "Hall of Fame" and had lunch in a Victorian house which our friend's mother, Mrs. Frank Goodyear, had given to the horse "Hall of Fame". Then we drove back to Augusta and joined the Brumms for dinner. On Friday, the Brumms watched the morning rounds and we the afternoon. Carol was worn out and we decided to try to get a plane out early Saturday to return home. We were lucky to get a flight because extra planes had been arranged to fly out players not making the Friday cut. We watched the final two days in the comfort of Carol's Den at 870 Lesley.

Knowing that I had chosen to be with Gary Player, who had won the PGA tournament at Aronomink in 1962, Dr. Whelan invited me to lunch and play his course soon after I returned in April. It was a wondrous day and I did my best to answer all questions about

Player, his fitness, his golf fundamentals, his family's unity, and the divided country he was representing in the "Wide World of Golf". Our discussions of world leaders, morality, and people (as patients), tended to add more permanence to our friendship.

Carol's late husband, Alexander "Sandy" Rush seldom golfed. Although he rarely played, he was popular enough to be elected to the Board of Directors of the Gulph Mills, Golf Club. This club had been started in 1916 by golfers who wanted to have a club where you did not have to have a tee time, as you needed to do, if you were a member of Philadelphia Country Club or Merion Golf. After "Sandy" Rush died in 1983, his good friend, Frank (Nank) D'Olier began to be active at Gulph Mills G.C., serving as Chairman of the House Committee. Carol's mother, stepfather, and her married sister were all members, but Carol, before 1985, played little golf. "Nank" suggested we apply to be golfing members. We were elected in late May 1985. At Gulph Mills, Wednesday was men's day. The members had a tradition of welcoming the members of Sunny Brook G.C., situated east of the Schuylkill River. G.M.G.C. members were welcomed to lunch and 18 hole low-ball of foursome competition on Thursdays. This was organized by John Brumley, assisted by Caleb and Bernie Fox. I recall joining each group once, before we set off on the 600 mile drive to Maine for the summer, Carol having an 1895 3 story house on the main street of the village of Northeast Harbor on Mount Desert Island, in 'Down East' Maine.

Sailing is the major activity of Northeast Harbor. Carol did not own a boat, but her friends were generous in inviting us to join them. Northeast Harbor Golf Club was started in 1895 with a 9 whole course. Since 1975, the summer professional has been Robert Gardner III of Chicago and Naples, Florida. Rob is the grandson of Robert Gardner, who eliminated the 14 year-old Bobby Jones in the third round of the U.S. Amateur held at Merion in 1916. Gardner was defeated in the 1916 finals by his fellow Chicagoan, Chick Evans, who had won the U.S. Open earlier that June. Rob's grandfather had a great Amateur career playing on the Walker Cup Team and competing in England in the early 20's. Our pro, Rob was a steady player, great teacher of the fundamentals, and superior in his knowledge of golf history. His great contribution was the organization of the weekly "scrambles" every Friday, with 60 to 64 men and women participating in low gross ball of foursome competition. In 1925, Jacob Disston, Philadelphia saw maker, donated enough acreage East of Sergeant Drive Northwest of the village, to make the course 18 holes, most of which are in the woods. In 1942-1945, only 9 holes were maintained, and the other 9 were restored only in the past 10 years, the momentum to do that having started with the club's (1995) "Centennial Board" decision to give the all year round citizens incentives to open up the overgrown fairways.

The Kebo Valley Golf Club course was laid out west of Bar Harbor in 1888. It is surrounded by the Acadia National Park. It is also a private club, but open to the public (for a high greens fee) for summer visitors. When Taft was President, the Course's 17th hole was in the national spotlight, when it was reported that Taft's score for the hole was in the high teens. Several foursomes from Northeast Harbor are members and play there several times a week. After the 4th July celebrations, Carol was determined to improve her short game and putting so we went to the club after breakfast every weekday morning and had pleasure in our improvement, which was evident in the "Scrambles" competitions on Fridays.

A letter from Curtis Person was forwarded from Villanova. Curtis had remarried and was living with his new wife, Meredith in North Carolina. The letter was an invitation to join them next June for a golfing tour of Western Ireland and in July fly to Glasgow for the British Open to be played at Turnberry in Ayrshire on the Irish Sea side of Scotland. Carol encouraged by her play, and liking Curtis, said, "Let's do it". So we asked to be included.

Soon it was June 1986. We drove to Northeast Harbor, and the house was open as Carol had previously arranged. Our travel agent had arranged for us to fly from Maine to Boston where we boarded the Aerlingus flight to Shannon in mid June. Meredith and Curtis met us at Shannon, some of the group being on our plane, whom we had not yet met. Curtis had arranged for the Ashford Castle van drivers to collect our clubs and baggage and we all rode the short distance from Shannon Airport, County Clare to Ashford. We learned that we were to stay at Ashford for several days until the entire golfing group was assembled; before being bused to the courses we were going to play in County Clare and County Kerry. We learned that Jack Mulcahy, an amateur golfing friend of Curtis, was the new owner of the Ashford Castle property.

By the dinner hour at the Castle, another group had arrived and we were joined at dinner by John Mulcahy. Mulcahy came to the US from Ireland as a young man, and built up a chemical company, very successful and profitable. He was going to live in Ireland and seek investments there. As Pfizer was expanding in the sixties, they bought Mulcahy's company and asked him to stay on. Because of his business acumen and personality, he was given greater responsibility and was paid well, usually with extra shares. So when he retired in the seventies his severance package made him a wealthy man. Later, we learned his sons had good jobs in American companies and when his wife died, he told his sons he was moving back to Ireland.

That evening we were told that the next day, when several of us thought we were going to play on the 6 hole, par 3 course, that the last group was yet to come and that the Waterville Golf Resort in S. Kerry "on the ring" was the ultimate destination. This was also owned by Mulcahy and was his Ireland home. His house was next to the practice range. On the second morning, we were all bused to Shannon, and there, picked up the final group. In as much as their plane had arrived late, the round at Lahinch was cancelled in order for us to cross the Shannon, and have lunch at the new Ballybunion Club House and then proceed on another three hour bus ride to Waterville, close to the Atlantic coast. After drinks and dinner accompanied by a young Irish woman playing Celtic airs on the harp, we retired early to prepare for a full day of Golf at Waterville. After morning golf, some of us had lunch in a pub in the village, a mile or so toward the Atlantic Coast. We were surprised to see a statue of Charlie Chaplin on the street. This was because he was a frequent vacationer there.

When we returned to the resort we learned that Curtis had arranged to have a bus take us from Waterville to golf at Ballybunion. After an early morning breakfast and a 2 hour plus bus ride we arrived at the club on the south bank of the Shannon close to where it entered the Atlantic. Although the new Ballybunion course designed by Robert Trent Jones was open, our tee times were on the "Old Course". The design of this and its history led to its designation as one of the top ten courses in the world as reported in George Peper's book "Golf in America". The day at Ballybunion was beautiful and Carol and I had a most enjoyable time, having young girl caddies and playing as a twosome. We were through the 18 holes of the "Old Course" early, having lost only a half dozen balls on the river holes. After lunch with some of our group, we decided to walk around the nearest holes of the new course. We had arranged with our girl caddies that they would help us get to the nearest holes. This was important because Jones' course designs usually had a distance from green to the next tee that was almost as far as the distance from tee to green. This was a comment made of his design of Spyglass Hill at Pebble Beach, California, one of the venues where the tourney called "The Crosby" is now played every year in late January or early February.

Ballybunion

After our play at Ballybunion we returned to Waterville for our last night's stay. Leaving early the next morning on one large bus, we arrived on schedule to board a plane to Glasgow, Scotland. There at the airport, we were met by the proprietor of the Band B in Ayrshire. Our clubs and baggage were sorted out and we piled into 4 vans and drove about an hours ride south to a house about 5 miles East of Turnberry. This was a Tuesday and most of us requested that we be driven over to Turnberry to watch the final practice round on Wednesday. We were met at the airport by the Band B operator. His home was about a 30 minute drive East of Turnberry in Airshire. Our good fortune was being assigned to stay in the Band B. This was the point at which all vehicles taking us to Turnberry started. Those not at the Band B. had rental cars. Our arrival there was in time for a siesta and then early dinner. There was some delay in serving dinner as the head man seemed to leave all details of getting us drinks and dinner to his wife and coworkers. He drank with the guests. During the dinner hour, there were enough of us who wanted to spend the last practice day at the Golf course. This was assured that evening. In 1977 I had stayed at the hotel and played the course, so I knew there was much to see.

Wednesday was a beautiful day. Carol had a Philadelphia golfing friend, a contemporary of her mother's, who was a member of the R and A (Royal and Ancient Golf Club). Carol told him in May, June about our plans and he promised Carol his tickets. Thursday it rained and we spent the day at the R & A Tent. Friday, Saturday and Sunday were beautiful days. On Sunday, after 9 holes, Greg Norman held on to win the event. Sunday evening dinner was the group's final get-together and Curtis and Meredith were complimented on the wonderful experience they created for us. After breakfast, Monday morning every couple was on their own.

Soon after meeting Curtis at the airport on our arrival at Shannon, he had told me he had a tee time to play the "Old Course" at Saint Andrews. He asked me if I would like to play in his foursome and we made plans to rent a car and stay at the golf course hotel on the edge of the "Old Course" road hole. We obtained a rental car Monday and drove east into Fife and Saint Andrews; where we were assigned a room overlooking one of the other courses but not the "Old Course". This was most pleasant, because, even in mid July, there was light to 10:30 – 11:00 p.m. So, before retiring, we saw several groups tee off from 8:00 – 9:00 p.m. We had an early breakfast on Tuesday and we went to the "Old Course" and were at the Starter's Shack at least one hour before the tee time Curtis mentioned. Awaiting me was a telegram from Curtis stating that their plan had changed and for me to use the tee time as I saw fit.

There were no other players ready to start at that early time. There was, however, an experienced caddy available. Carol said she wanted to walk along the "old course" layout with me. My only memory is that it was a beautiful day, the caddy was competent and humorous, and I hit more good shots and lost fewer balls than when, in 1977, Lucinda walked around with me. I always admired Carol's willingness to share with me the disappointment of not having Curtis with me. Sometime in the next four or five years, I was in Baltimore attending a reunion of Hopkins Medical graduates. I noticed that the M.D. signing the attendance roster, jot down Memphis as his home town. I told him I had a friend from Memphis named Curtis Person. This M.D. became very excited and said in loud tones, "Curtis is a patient of mine and he is the worst patient I have ever had – he does not do one thing I urge him to do.

We returned to the hotel, checked out, and drove into the village. After lunch there, we visited several of the shops of which there were many with attractive golf outfits, but expensive! The store that attracted Carol was where all the clan tartans were on sale. Her father was Stanley MacDonald Smith so she purchased a MacDonald tartan. I then told her I wanted to go to Muirfield where I knew of an attractive inn near the Muirfield club house. This inn was designed by the architect who had laid out New Delhi in India for the British. When I was at Muirfield in 1977 this place had been fully booked and we moved on. We drove there, parked the car in the Muirfield club parking lot, and walked over to the hotel and asked to be shown rooms that were available. There were vacancies and Carol picked out a room overlooking Muirfield's 18th green and fairway. We then walked back to the club house and entered the office of the secretary/starter. I told him I was staying at the inn "Grey Walls," was alone, and wanted to fit in with a group to be a foursome. He said there was nothing that afternoon, but on the next morning, a group of Canadians had tee times. He could not find a record of the names of all in the group but if there were not 16 players to make 4 foursomes, and, if it was agreeable with their leader, perhaps I might join the uneven group. Encouraged by this, we drove around the area and I showed Carol courses I played in 1984 when I was there with "wide world golfers". I remember the pleasure I had enjoyed in July 1984, playing North Berwick, a course noted for the design of an elevated green on a par 3 hole. The next morning we were up early, had a good Scottish breakfast, I retrieved my clubs from the rental car, and we walked over to the Muirfield Club's practice green near the first tee. Carol had her putter and so, with no one around, we putted for about 30 minutes before players began to arrive.

It was then that I approached several men asking if they were Canadians. I must have accosted 4 or 5 before I found a Canadian. He assented to my request to be introduced to their group leader. As it turned out they didn't have 4 complete foursomes. I gave the leader my Philadelphia handicap, he reshuffled his cards, and I played with men whose handicaps were above 25. The wind was coming off the Firth of Forth and the rough was high. My caddy and I lost quite a few balls, but I played Muirfield, and Carol, good sport that she was, followed our foursome inconspicuously. I did not play well but I was not the poorest player in our foursome. They were all pleasant and I was glad I was there and able to join them.

We had lunch, drove back to Prestwick, and obtained seats on the evening British Air to Boston. There we were able to get an early morning flight to Bangor and, after about a 75 minute drive to Northeast Harbor, were back at 11 Harborside Road by noon. What do you think we did after lunch? First we went to the golf club, found there were still two openings for the Friday "scrambles," and played a few holes on the gorgeous, late July day. Then we went back to the village, did some shopping and Carol made a few phone calls, "we are back - please join us for drinks and dinner on the 28th." It would be Carol's 65th birthday, her daughters and families were coming so a celebration was mandatory.

We played golf at Northeast Harbor almost every weekday in August and September. There was great improvement in Carol's accuracy and distance off the tees. My short game and putting continued to improve. Carol's teams in the scrambles were winning prizes almost every week. I was more confident about my consistency and I was looking forward to the alternate shot competition at Merion Golf Club on the last Friday in September. The weather in early September was unusually good and Carol was reluctant to leave Maine. Carol's mother's 97th birthday was 9/15/86 and so we drove down to Philadelphia on the day before going to visit her at 4-5 pm at her home on Lesley Road. She was miserable, having suffered a paralyzing stroke at the age of 93 but was happy to see Carol. I learned that my application to be an "overseas" member of Ballybunion was accepted. With the news that I was granted a lifetime membership for an initiation fee of $250, I discovered that Carol did not have to have a separate membership. Their rules stated a member's wife could be the husband's guest, paying the usual daily greens fee.

I discussed another trip to Ireland in 1987 with Carol to pick out the Ballybunion green jacket included in the initiation fee but Carol said, "You go by yourself. My daughters have promised to come with their families on my birthday, so that might be a good time for you to make the Ballybunion trip." May and June were busy times socially for Carol and me with little time for golf. We left Villanova for Maine after attending my 50th reunion at Swarthmore.

I left on the second Saturday for Boston and Shannon on Aerlingus, arriving at 6 am. I had no trouble getting a rental car. My plan was to drive west in County Clare, staying North of the Shannon. The course known as Lahinch was on the Atlantic coast near a small village. In the parking lot was a local member putting on his shoes to play. Having heard that the course had several "blind holes" and "crossing fairways", I asked him if I could join him so that he could steer me around the course. We had a most pleasant time, the sun was out and I said goodbye sometime before noon, thanking him profusely. I found my way to the ferry terminal for the trip south across the Shannon and, in less than an hour, the boat arrived, and was soon loaded for the half hour trip across the wide river. This landed me in County Kerry about 30 miles East of Ballybunion and was quite near the harbor where the Pan-American clipper ships landed. I found my rooming house easily, and, having had nothing to eat after landing at Shannon, I went to the Ballybunion golf clubhouse for lunch. After lunch, I sought out the club secretary, Sean Walsh. One of my lunch waiters, when asked if Sean ever came to the club on Sundays, replied that he had seen him earlier in the day and that he seemed very busy or preoccupied.

I found his office in the new club house and he was most welcoming, taking me into a cloak room where there was a rack of Ballybunion jackets. My initiation fee included one. The jacket selection was minimal and his best effort was to fit me with a jacket, which was a bit tight but the rest of the lot were all too large. He told me about the arrival early the next day of a prominent American visitor who would be able to play on the shorter "Old Course", only if he could have a motor cart. Walsh said he had arranged with John Mulcahy to have one of the Waterville carts put on a truck and hauled up to Ballybunion early Monday. I asked who the visitor might be, and he replied, "Tip O'Neill." A congressman from New Jersey, who was an overseas member, was O'Neill's host and the group was given a tee time of 1pm on Monday.

I played early in the morning, joining a threesome at 0800, and had an early lunch. There was an unusually large crowd for a Monday and I watched O'Neill and his foursome tee off. It struck me that O'Neill was an infrequent player and this was a "ceremonial" or public affairs match for the well-liked minority leader of the Congress. After the round, O'Neill allowed me to take several snapshots which I gave to the few Democrats in Carol's circle at Northeast Harbor. I stayed several more days at Ballybunion, in order to get lodging at a B and B in County Sligo. I asked for directions about the most scenic route to take and how to return to Shannon by another route to make my western crossing the last day of July. I had two major desires, one to play the outstanding course layout of the County Sligo Golf Club, parallel to the mountain that W.B. Yeats had described in his writings. I played the course several times meeting several locals who were all great hosts. They took pictures of me with the mountain, Benbulben, in the background. It was in their pro shop that I was attracted to their green tie, which I purchased.

On 28th July 1987, Carol had her 66th birthday. Her daughters, Molly and Sandra were there with their children. Bill Purdy, Molly's husband, a pediatrician by training, plays golf, and, when in Maine, joins the Northeast Golf Club Friday scrambles. Bill is a good golfer, and when in the scrambles, his foursome usually posts the lowest score. Their house in Durham is on a golf course. He has enjoyed playing the Merion East Course with contemporaries who are members. In 2004, his application for a non-resident membership was submitted and approved. I believe because of higher education costs of his three adult children, he has sought to defer accepting that invitation.

8/21/87 was the date of the NEHGC Scrambles. This was a memorable afternoon. Our foursome was Janny Jackson, her son Gardner, and John Adams, who grew up in Northeast Harbor, and started as a caddy on the course. We played twelve holes and par was 43. Our score was "Even Threes;" 36 or 7 under. There was a Men's Day event during which we played 15 holes and, in our foursome was a guest from California. Others were Charles Dickey and Bill Wistar, both from Philadelphia, but long-time members of NEGHC. We posted a 45: even 3's. We remained in Maine until late September; returning just before the last Friday so I could participate in the 7th Anniversary of R.T. Jones Memorial Alternate Shot Event. started in 1980 to celebrate the 50th Anniversary of the 1930 U.S Amateur at Merion. This was Jones 4th major win in 1930 and some golf writers referred to it as "The Grand Slam". My first opportunity to compete in this alternate shot event was in 1984 and the competition was held each year on the last Friday of September. I had played in a similar format at the SFGC after its Muirfield Lunch and enjoyed the format and the opportunity it gave to socialize. In 1990 I met my partner, Graham King, at lunch and learned he was a low handicap player, between 5 and 12. My handicap (30) was high as my prowess was more in chipping and putting. Many of the Par 3's on the East course are odd-numbered holes. When I asked Graham what he was able to do with his tee shot on the par 3's, he replied, "I'm usually on the green, but often not near the pin." I suggested that he tee off on the odd-numbered holes that day. He was on the green on every odd numbered par 3 with his tee shot. My good fortune was to hole in several birdie putts. We posted the lowest handicap score. In the1996 Jones Event, I was paired with Gary Baum. Having played in foursome breakfast events with him, I knew that Gary, a low handicap player, was consistent with his tee shots. He liked to tee off on the odd holes when we played together. However, we learned from the starter, that we were in a foursome scheduled to begin on the 18th hole. This is a difficult hole because the tee shot must carry a ravine in order to reach the fairway. My poor first and third shots caused us to post a 10 on that hole. When we learned that our score was the 1996 low handicap total of the day, we were surprised, and my name went on the plaque for the second time.

Our golfing in 1988 was in the desert area of southern California. We were guests of S.F.G.C President, George Cronin and his wife at Smoke Tree Resort. George and I played one of the older 18 hole courses in old Palm Springs. We were with them only a few days as we were en route to board the Sea Cloud for a whale-watching visit to the Pacific side of Baja California.

Our oldest grand daughter, Erin was 5 in April. Her mother had an architects' meeting in Boston, and she inquired when Carol planned to go to Maine. We had an invitation from our friend, Janey Jackson, a golfing widow, to be her house guest in mid June at Dedham. Her son, Gardner, had obtained tickets as he was on the committee to stage the US Open at the Brookline Country Club. We arranged with Cynthia to meet her and Erin in Boston. Cynthia then was free to attend her meeting and we would look after Erin and return her to Cynthia in Boston, when we were expected to be with Janey in Dedham. We were there on Tuesday and Wednesday and walked the course for the practice rounds. I tried to do this for the first round on Thursday but my knees were swollen and painful. Carol drove us back to Wayne so I could get help from Dr. Good. We watched the event on the TV as Curtis Strange won on Sunday. He repeated his win the next year at Oak Hill in Rochester, thus being one golfer who won the US Open in successive years. Dr. Good drained the fluid out of both my knees. He suggested that I was a "good candidate" for total knee replacement. He was very patient with me over the next ten years. In May 1999, he replaced my right knee with excellent results which lasted until 15 May 2007.

In 1989 I was asked to assist the Transportation committee for the USGA Amateur Championship at Merion. My Assignment began on Sunday and was from 7 am to 1 pm. I was to assign golf carts to USGA officials whose names were on the duty list for a specific time and location. This was pleasant to do although, as predicted by the Merion member who selected me, some aggressive USGA volunteers tried to get them when they had "No Assigned

Duties". The USGA President then was a fellow member of S.F.G.C. he (Grant Spaeth) was at Merion and asked me to take him out to Swarthmore where his father, Carl Spaeth rented a faculty house during World War II. This was a very pleasant afternoon and Grant mentioned it when I see him later in California. Chris Patton won the Amateur in 1989 but never made it in the pro ranks.

Carol had a memorial service for her mother at St. Davids Church Radnor PA in early January. Mrs. Hollingsworth was 101 when she died 31 Dec 1990. Carol came first to San Francisco and we played a round there at SFGC on Thursday (ladies day). Then we went to Palm Springs. This was a busy week of instruction and much individual attention without any attempt to make over your game. .

In May of 1993 we made the decision to apply for a Villa at Beaumont. The summer was spent at Northeast Harbor with the Friday Scrambles at NEHGC the golfing highlight. In September the Ballybunion Golf Club invited overseas members to join them by forming a three man team of men and women in "Low Ball of Threesome Net Competition." Carol was placed with two Irish woman members. I had no partners until the tournament committee matched me with an overseas member, Tom Aiken from New Jersey, a member of Pine Valley. The Irish member had a high handicap as I did but he played as well as Tom and our team placed second, losing to an Irish player and two Merion Golf Club Members. Carol and I brought back to Northeast Harbor Waterford Crystal replicas of club heads and pleasant memories of Irish hospitality.

Carol's favorite nephew, R. Stockton Rush, had a new wife and was living in San Francisco. They invited us to join them in 1994 and we arranged to go there the last two weeks in February. Stockton, Carol and I played golf at SFGC and his new wife, Jinkie, walked around the course in her bare feet. Stockton enjoyed the outing as he played well and talked about applying for membership. The last Saturday of February was the annual alternate shot competition and I played in that and was on the winning "Drake" team, having won more matches than the "Wellingtons."

That summer at Northeast Harbor we played almost every day with the object being to do well for our assigned team in the Friday scrambles. Carol was usually a winner of one of the four prizes because of her fairway tee shots, good short game and putting. The season closed with the Thursday luncheon meeting of the Pot and Kettle Club, whose first woman speaker was an executive of one of the New York advertising agencies. By the fall my blood pressure was high enough to warrant treatment and my knees were swollen from osteoarthritis. Dr.Good was removing fluid from my knees every two or three months. When I was well enough to play, I would go either to Gulph Mills; or Merion on Wednesday and Saturday and tried to play at Sunny Brook every Thursday. The highlight of our visit to NEH was the Friday scrambles on July 28th; Carol's team won first prize being two under par. This was Carol's 74th and she was very pleased.

In April we were fortunate to have the Whelans as our guests at the Merion Golf Club as a celebration of my 80th birthday. That summer at Northeast Harbor we were at the golf course nearly every day with an occasional lunch invitation on a powerboat owned by one of Carol's friends. We left Maine in beautiful weather and Carol agreed to have me back in time for the last Friday for the Bobby Jones Memorial competition. Before the end of the year I lost my Merion golfing buddy, Frank Itgen from stomach cancer.

In February of 1997 at SFGC I played in the British day of golf. The Swarthmore College Alumni Association sponsored a trip in April featuring the showplaces of the Hudson Valley Historical Society. We drove there visiting for the second time the hometown of my father in Cold Spring. We then drove to the hotel in White Plains area which was our headquarters as we visited different houses each morning and afternoon for four days. This was a pleasant tour with many "old" Swarthmore friends in the group.

Carol joined me in meeting my 1937 classmates for my 60th Reunion on the Swarthmore campus in June. Although I usually joined the golf outing at the nearby golf club in prior years, I decided not to do that so Carol might be able to visit some newer classmates at the luncheon on the campus in the new Kohlberg building. What was most pleasant was that Nancy and Jim Buckingham came from

New York and we sat together at lunch. Soon after that weekend we set off for Maine; earlier than we usually made the trip and were rewarded by good weather and the golf course was dryer than it usually was in mid June. We played every day.

In January 1998 the weather was cold and ice was often on the walkways in the middle of the day. My knees were bothersome with fluid in both knee joints. Having been a patient of Dr.Good for almost 10 years, he would drain the fluid and replace that with Cortisone. This was always administered with the statement, "You would be an excellent candidate for total knee joint replacement." Carol's 50 year house was beginning to cause her distress with flooding of the basement and toilet drainage problems. Thus, when I suggested, "Let's go to California," She readily agreed. This we did in mid February. The weather was good; we had a rental car and went to SFGC on Tuesdays and Thursdays (ladies days). I was able to play 9 holes at first and then 36 on the last Saturday (British Golf Day). When we returned to Villanova in March the weather was better and we played 9 holes at Gulph Mills G.C. three or four times weekly. We went to Maine in June and stayed there until late September playing golf almost every day. The autumn and early winter went by quickly.

We were looking forward to January 1999 having booked our fourth trip on the Sea Cloud for a garden trip beginning in the Barbados. This was to be lead by Patrick Bowes, an Irish Expert, and was attended by many members of the NYC chapter of the Garden Club of America. This was a great trip and I was concerned about whether I should have one knee replaced. Carol agreed to go to California with me in February and we visited Stockton and Jinkie Rush in San Francisco. Carol stayed several days with them while I moved on to the Sequoias. My primary physician suggested a consultation with an Orthopedist at the Palo Alto Medical Foundation. I saw Dr. Lannin the next day at the clinic. He agreed that I was a good candidate and suggested that the right knee should be done first. He hand an opening in his operating schedule in August. I let him know that I was still living in Philadelphia and would continue under the care of Dr. Good rather than having the surgery at that time.

Back in Villanova, I saw Dr. Good again and he gave me an operating date and on May 26 the joint was replaced at Bryn Mawr Hospital with subsequent rehab at Paoli. We went to Maine in June and I saw a therapist there three times weekly and walked on the course at NEHGC while Carol played. On July 16th I began to swing a club again and played in my first Scrambles on August 16th. Our team came in second. We stayed in Maine until September 30th as my walking and golf play continued to improve. After returning to Philadelphia I resumed golfing at Merion, usually playing with Bob Castner, whom I met there in 1987. The autumn passed quickly and we accepted the invitation of the Purdy family to spend Christmas week with them in Durham, N.C. Their house was on a golf course and, on several good weather days there, we played the 3 holes nearest their house.

We returned to Philadelphia to join Sarah Lee and Bill Stokes to be their guests at the City Troup Ball on New Year's Eve. I attempted to dance but my legs did not move the way I thought they should. The evening otherwise was most pleasant. As the new century began, the problems with Carol's 870 Lesley Road house maintenance continued. She said yes to every villa and apartment she was shown at the Beaumont except two, one of which had in the lower level a swimming pool, and the other a movie theater. My other knee was bothersome but, with time, I seemed to have less trouble with the left knee and the right was much better after the replacement. In April, I played in an 18 hole East Course breakfast tournament and my golfing was more fun then than it had been for the prior 10 years. My medical problems were now skin cancers on my face which I had removed at Lankenau before we left for Maine in early June. I always wore a broad brimmed hat on the golf course and in the NEH pool when I walked in the water during noon hour. We golfed every day and this paid off for me. On Friday, 18 August 2000 in the scrambles our team came in first, posting a 2 under par score. We returned to Villanova from Maine in time for me to participate in the Sept. 29 Friday Memorial Jones tournament. My routine was to ask Carol if she wanted to play at Gulph Mills and, if not, I would play at Merion or Sunnybrook. At Christmas we visited the Purdys and played golf on the three holes near their house on sunny days with all the family participating.

After returning to Villanova in late April, I was invited to play golf in Maine for the Northeast Harbor fund raiser at the Bar Harbor course on the mainland near Ellsworth. Carol was not willing to go to Maine that early as it was then raining in the northeast. She did, however, arrange to have the house opened and I was to be on my own for meals. I managed satisfactorily and the rain stopped two days before the start of the tournament. Play went on even though the course was flooded in some areas. I met all the locals who had sponsored the tournament, and, although my golf was poor, I was made to feel good about making the effort to support the event.

In June the weather warmed, the sun dried out the Northeast Harbor course and I was able to get around using the Buick Skylark that we garaged there over the winter. Carol arrived in mid June and by then she was able to play the course with me and she was happy to be in the modernized 1895 house which her daughters had insisted on renovating with modern appliances in the bathroom and kitchen. I kept busy when not on the golf course by getting rid of the clutter in the basement and picking up the fallen branches in the side yard which the local gardeners hauled away.

SFGC 1993 With Stan Madden and Ian

In March 2004 when I paid my annual dues, I decided to resign from Merion where I had belonged since 1958. This was primarily because my golf and bridge-playing member friends were either dying or unable to play. That summer in Maine I played less golf with Carol; she preferred playing with a woman who was her next door neighbor there.

9. Return to California: 2006

While recuperating from my May 1999 complete right knee replacement, I had the opportunity to request senior status at San Francisco Golf Club. This was granted in 2000 by the Board of Directors. Not knowing how much golf I might be able to play after the knee replacement, I was comfortable with my new status of being able to use the practice range, putting greens and clubhouse amenities. I did not play the beautiful 18 hole course nor host guest play.

Golf with Joe, Cyn and Alex

With my change of residence in the Philadelphia area in late 2005 to the Sequoias in Portola Valley, I was fortunate enough to host a luncheon on April 2, 2006 to celebrate my 90th birthday with family and fellow Sequoia golfers. Easter brunch in 2006 with Gary Harmon and the Kruegers was most enjoyable as well as the 2007 Easter buffet with my family.

In the 90's a putting green, complete with sand hazards was installed near the bowling green and the swimming pool at the Sequoias. Residents, June and Dick Fitzsimmons have led the group of golfers in staging an annual putting contest not only for experienced residents, but also for beginners with handicapping in order to make prize-winning possible for all. Tee times have been arranged weekly

Sequoias Golfers

for 9 hole play at the Sunnyvale Municipal Course. Usually there are two foursomes and these have included both Fitzsimmons, both Olsons, Judy Speidel, Mary Brown Lawrence, John Donegan, Dr. Duncan Govan, Jim Malloch, Howard Middleton, and Marty Tarshes. Players on the resident waiting list are welcome and we have also enjoyed the company of Ladera resident, Dan Grey. The course is laid out in what was once a quarry and has 7 par 3, and 2 par 4 holes. Play is pleasant and timely. Few balls are lost. We generally start at 9 AM and are usually finished by 11 AM.

10. Reflections: Serious Thoughts on the Game of Golf

By definition, golf is a game in which each player uses a number of golf clubs to hit a small white ball into a succession of holes, usually 9 or 18 in number, situated at various distances over a course having natural or artificial obstacles; the object being to get the ball into each hole in as few strokes as possible. Any given course is usually on 125 to 175 acres. There are exceptions. The Merion Golf Club East Course was, I believe, laid out on less than 100 acres in 1912, by Hugh Wilson. If the course is bordered by salt water, such as St. Andrew's in Fife, Scotland, it might be termed a links course.

The game, in my opinion, is the greatest because it tests ones motor and intellectual assets, requires patience, curiosity, inventiveness and a sense of anticipation. My own experience is that I have never left the last green of a given round without the belief and anticipation that in my next game, whether tomorrow or next week, I might be able to play better and score less.

Motor skills may be developed early, as suggested by pictures of the swing of 3 year old Tiger Woods made when his father, Earl, arranged for him to be shown on the stage of the Ed Sullivan Vaudeville Show in the late 20th century. Now Tiger's game is one of the best in the world, even though in the 2007 US Open at Oakmont, Pittsburgh, PA, he was unable to hit his approach shots close enough to the hole and was unable to make the necessary one put to par the holes remaining. He lost the tournament to Angel Cabrera of Argentina, whose score for the four rounds was under par. Tiger Woods was tied by Jim Furyk 2 strokes behind.

In the game of golf, what is par? Par is the number of strokes set as a standard for a hole, frequently four, or par for the 18 hole course, frequently 72 for 18 holes. "Golf, the Greatest Game", is the title of a recent book on the victory of the amateur and one time caddy, Francis Ouimet, over two famous English golf pros, Vardon and Ray, at the U.S.G.A. Open at The Country Club at Brookline in 1913. Many will agree with me, but some cynics have said that it is 'a good walk spoiled.'

The game has been called "Royal and Ancient." I do not know how the game started, but I like to think that the "Royal and Ancient" term refers to the role that the club with this name, whose HQ is near the first tee of the "old course" at St. Andrew's, refers to the influence of that club, recently with the cooperation of the U.S.G.A., has played in standardizing the rules of play. The crux of the game is to hit the ball "far and sure." This motto was inscribed on the door of the Saint Andrew's House of the famous Scottish caddy player. He was paired with Royalty to win an important- "high stakes" challenge match in Scotland in the 1700s. "Far and Sure" means distance and accuracy, and has been the logo of the Northeast Harbor Golf Club on Mount Desert Island, Maine, since its start in 1895, if my information from that club's professional, Robert Gardner III, is correct.

11. Suggestions For An Aspiring Golfer

1. Start as young as possible. Tiger Woods is the best example. His father was much like a professional golf coach. He entered his son in junior competitions. His success in these led to his playing after leaving the under 16 group to National Amateur Events. Tiger's success in these match play events was remarkable. In the USGA National Amateur Competition, he won this event three years in a row. In several of these that I watched, he was behind until he evened the match in the 16th or 17th hole to go on and win the match. He then enrolled at Stanford, which had built its own 18 hole course in 1930. It was in his third year there that he decided to turn pro. Since then he has established a record of PGA and major wins that suggest he will, one day, equal or surpass Jack Nicklaus majors of 18 wins, including his one USGA Amateur title.

Another example is Michelle Wie of South Korean heritage, living in the Hawaiian Islands. Because of her athletic stature and swing she has turned pro (for commercial contracts) even though she has never won a major golfing event. She will enter Stanford in the fall semester of 2007 but will not be eligible for intercollegiate events.

2. Get the benefit of the expertise of an experienced golf instructor. This costs money but it saves time and is a better buy than cigarettes, gasoline, alcohol, or fancy clothes. The only more necessary expenditures are soap, water, clean clothes and education.

3. Join the most favorable golf club. By the nature of this expense, this is a family decision. Usually the family has a membership and a junior golf program is an asset of most clubs.

4. Select a fellow member as your model and/or mentor. This will, if properly approached, lead to meeting other members and perhaps some playing lessons and suggestions.

5. Establish your club handicap as soon as possible. This means you must count every swing, write your score on every hole of the course card and post the record of each and every round. With serious attention to practice and play, one should be able to lower the handicap (usually 36 for beginners), one stroke monthly. This means one should be at 24 after a year. After 2 years, 18, 3 years, 15. With my own haphazard approach, I never had a handicap lower than 18. Also if I had posted a score under 100 in the last 20 years, I was pleased. In the past two years, playing 9 holes on a par 3 layout (with only two par 4s), my usual scores were between 40 and 45. One day, with lucky putting, I had a 36 for 9 holes. Having that round kept me playing eagerly until May 15, 2007. It was on this day that I had pain in my left knee and noted it was swollen, so I consulted my internist and an orthopedic surgeon. This led to x-ray evidence of fluid in my left knee joint and little cartilage remaining.

12. Further Reflections

Having been advised by our family friend, Steve Whelan Jr., to get my thoughts on paper, I was struggling in my 28th post-operative week to make my essay less wordy and more incisive. My son, Tom is helping, and I am encouraged.

On Monday April 7, 2008 the Wall Street Journal Report on Golf published J.P. Newport's summary, "How To Behave On The Golf Course." Upon reading this I realized that it summarized many of my own experiences. What follows is my own attempt to summarize for younger family members suggestions about the game that I have learned over the years.

Principle #1 Learn How To Shout "Fore." If you are not paying attention golf can be dangerous. To this day, I never know when a shot I planned to go one way is going to where I want it to go.

Principle #2 Follow the Golden Rule Whatever enables you to play your best against the course (which is your true opponent); you should also want for those playing with you. If this does not happen, the game ceases to be fun.

Principle #3 Know A Few Rules Basic is "Play the ball as it lies." Having been a member of the USGA, I was sent each year their booklet of updated rules which I have tried to follow. Newport, in his article, mentions "Golf and Etiquette Crystal Clear" by Yves Ton-That. This should help, particularly the rules bearing on what governs your play when you can't find your ball.

Principle #4 Keep Up! "Slow play is golf's biggest buzz kill." Be ready to hit when it is your turn.

Principle #5 Ask Questions. This record of what the game has meant to me is the collection of answers to that question that I began at age 10 and continue to ask, namely "How do expert golfers consistently hit the ball so close to the flag, and how do great putters, such as my heroes, Horton Smith and Bob Jones, get the ball into the hole.

Newport Concludes: "Golf as an industry does not do as much as it should to make newcomers feel welcome, but most individuals will be eager to help. Believe me, as long as you yell, 'Fore,' we're all happy to see you."

Appendix I. Hafkenschiel Ancestry

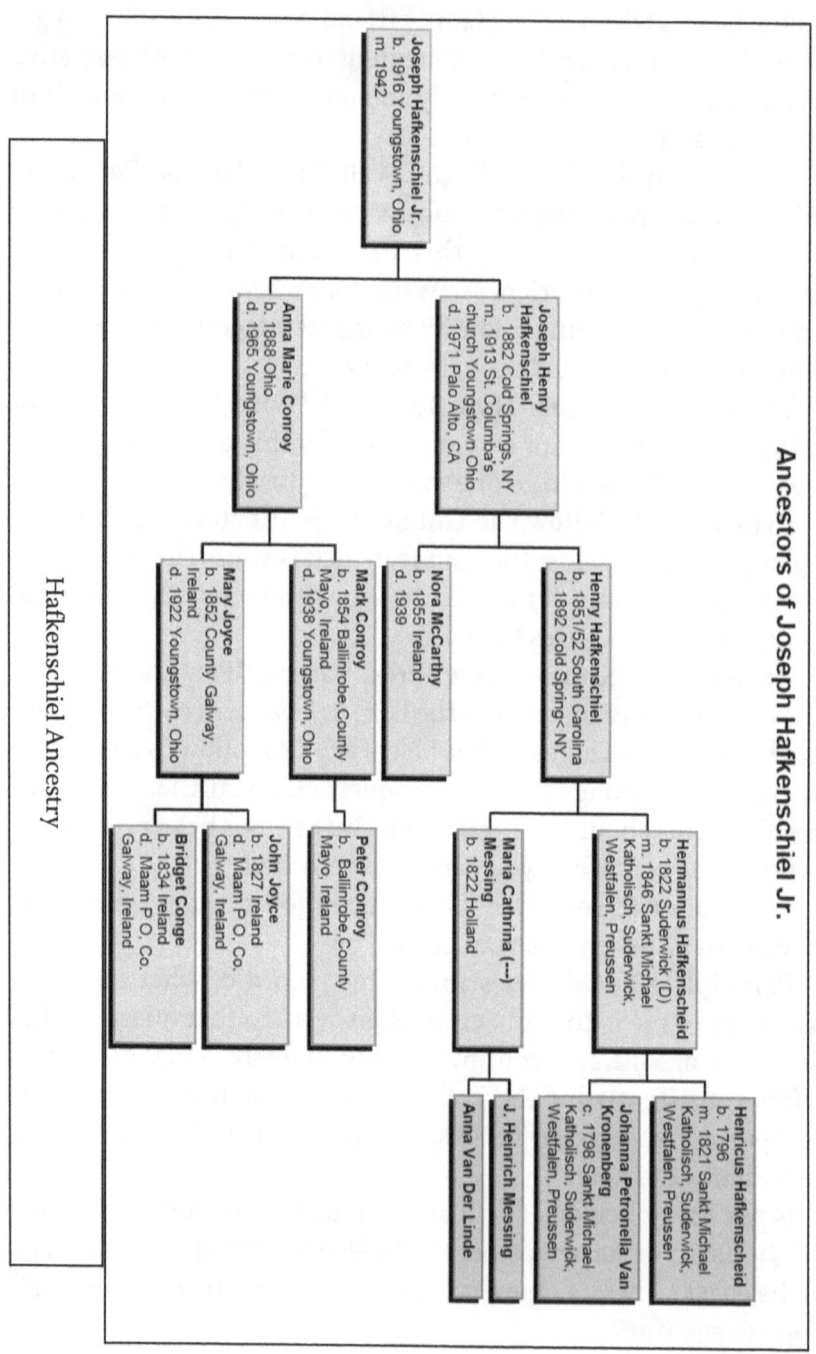

Ancestors of Joseph Hafkenschiel Jr.

Hafkenschiel Ancestry

Joseph Hafkenschiel Jr.
b. 1916 Youngstown, Ohio
m. 1942

Anna Marie Conroy
b. 1888 Ohio
d. 1965 Youngstown, Ohio

Joseph Henry Hafkenschiel
b. 1882 Cold Springs, NY
m. 1913 St. Columba's church Youngstown Ohio
d. 1971 Palo Alto, CA

Mary Joyce
b. 1852 County Galway,
d. 1922 Youngstown, Ohio
Ireland

Mark Conroy
b. 1854 Ballinrobe, County
Mayo, Ireland
d. 1938 Youngstown, Ohio

Nora McCarthy
b. 1855 Ireland
d. 1939

Henry Hafkenschiel
b. 1851/52 South Carolina
d. 1892 Cold Springs, NY

Bridget Conge
b. 1834 Ireland
d. Maam P.O. Co.
Galway, Ireland

John Joyce
b. 1827 Ireland
d. Maam P.O. Co.
Galway, Ireland

Peter Conroy
b. Ballinrobe, County
Mayo, Ireland

Maria Cathrina (---) Messing
b. 1822 Holland

Hermannus Hafkenscheid
b. 1822 Suderwick (D)
m. 1846 Sankt Michael
Katholisch, Suderwick,
Westfalen, Preussen

Anna Van Der Linde

J. Heinrich Messing

Johanna Petronella Van Kronenberg
c. 1798 Sankt Michael
Katholisch, Suderwick,
Westfalen, Preussen

Henricus Hafkenscheid
b. 1796
m. 1821 Sankt Michael
Katholisch, Suderwick,
Westfalen, Preussen

188

Appendix II. Ancestors of Joseph Hafkenschiel Jr.

1. **Joseph**[1] **Hafkenschiel Jr.**, born 2 Apr 1916 in Youngstown, Ohio, son of 2. Joseph Henry Hafkenschiel and 3. Anna Marie Conroy. He married on 18 Jul 1942 **Lucinda Buchanan Thomas**, born 11 May 1912 in Philadelphia, PA; died 16 Jan 1983 in Palo Alto, CA, daughter of Benjamin Abraham Thomas and Lucinda Buchanan Stackhouse.

Generation 2

2. **Joseph Henry**[2] **Hafkenschiel**, born 1882 in Cold Springs, NY; died 2 Aug 1971 in Palo Alto, CA, son of 4. Henry Hafkenschiel and 5. Nora McCarthy. He married on 1 Sep 1913 in St. Columba's church Youngstown Ohio 3. **Anna Marie Conroy**, born 20 Jul 1888 in Ohio; died Dec 1965 in Youngstown, Ohio, daughter of 6. Mark Conroy and 7. Mary Joyce.

Children of Joseph Henry Hafkenschiel and Anna Marie Conroy were as follows:

1   i   **Joseph**[1] **Hafkenschiel Jr.**, born 2 Apr 1916 in Youngstown, Ohio. He married on 18 Jul 1942 **Lucinda Buchanan Thomas**, born 11 May 1912 in Philadelphia, PA; died 16 Jan 1983 in Palo Alto, CA, daughter of Benjamin Abraham Thomas and Lucinda Buchanan Stackhouse.

  ii **Robert C.**[1] **Hafkenschiel**[1], born 27 Jan 1918 in Youngstown, Ohio; died 30 Mar 1925 in Youngstown, Ohio. Notes: Died of intestinal volvulus

---

1   Ohio Deaths .

Generation 3

4. Henry³ Hafkenschiel², born 1851/52 in South Carolina; died 9 Sep 1892 in Cold Spring< NY, son of 8. Hermannus Hafkenscheid and 9. Maria Cathrina (---) Messing. He married 5. **Nora McCarthy**, born Dec 1855 in Ireland; died 29 Mar 1939.

Notes for Henry Hafkenschiel
    Worked as barber.
Notes for Nora McCarthy
    Was a widow at age 44 Came to US in 1870. Both parents born in Ireland. Listed in 1900 census as Nora Hafkenchild.

Children of Henry Hafkenschiel and Nora McCarthy were as follows:

2   i **Joseph Henry² Hafkenschiel**, born 1882 in Cold Springs, NY; died 2 Aug 1971 in Palo Alto, CA. He married on 1 Sep 1913 in St. Columba's church Youngstown Ohio **Anna Marie Conroy**, born 20 Jul 1888 in Ohio; died Dec 1965 in Youngstown, Ohio, daughter of Mark Conroy and Mary Joyce.

    ii **Herman C.² Hafkenschiel**, born Feb 1884 in New York; died 22 Aug 1905 in Cold Spring, Ny.

    iii **Unknown² Hafkenschiel**.

6. Mark³ Conroy³, born 11 Mar 1854 in Ballinrobe,County Mayo, Ireland; died 26 Jan 1938 in Youngstown, Ohio, son of 10. Peter Conroy. He married 7. **Mary Joyce⁴**, born 8 Sep 1852 in County

---

2   1860 US Census . "Name: Herman Hafkenschield Residence: Charleston, South Carolina Minor civil division: 6th Ward Charleston City Age: 10 years Estimated birth year: 1850 Birth place: South Carolina Gender: Male Page: 1 Family number: 2 Film number: 805216 Digital GS number: 4296156 Image number: 00450 NARA publication number: M653 Collection: 1860 United States Census". "Name: Henry Hafkenschield Residence: Charleston, South Carolina Minor civil division: 6th Ward Charleston City Age: 8 years Estimated birth year: 1852 Birth place: South Carolina Gender: Male Page: 1 Family number: 2 Film number: 805216 Digital GS number: 4296156 Image number: 00450 NARA publication number: M653 Collection: 1860 United States Census".
3   Ohio Deaths .
4   Ibid.

Galway, Ireland; died 21 Apr 1922 in Youngstown, Ohio, daughter of 11. John Joyce and 12. Bridget Conge.

Notes for Mark Conroy

Emigrated in 1873, Both parents born in Ireland. Worked as peddler
Children: Ages in 1900
Mary 21
Margaret 18
Nora 14
Anna 10
Agnes 9
Frances 8
Mark 6
John 3
Naturalized in probate court Mahoning County Ohio in 1883

Notes for Mary Joyce

Immigrated 1880, Lived in Youngstown ward 6, had 11 children, with 9 living. Died of acute nephritis

Children of Mark Conroy and Mary Joyce were as follows:
i **Mary**^{2} **Conroy**, born 27 Nov 1877 in County Galway Ireland.
ii **Bridget**^{2} **Conroy**, born 27 Apr 1879.
iii **Geraldine**^{2} **Conroy**[5], born 26 Apr 1880. She married **Martin Carr.**
iv **Margaret**^{2} **Conroy**, born 5 Jul 1881.
v **Barbara F.**^{2} **Conroy**, born 18 Jul 1883.
vi **Nora**^{2} **Conroy**, born Feb 1886 in Ohio.
vii **Patrick**^{2} **Conroy**, born 6 Nov 1886.
3 viii **Anna**^{2} **Marie Conroy**, born 20 Jul 1888 in Ohio; died Dec 1965 in Youngstown, Ohio. She married on 1 Sep 1913 in St. Columba's church Youngstown Ohio **Joseph Henry Hafkenschiel**, born 1882 in Cold Springs, NY; died 2 Aug 1971 in Palo Alto, CA, son of Henry Hafkenschiel and Nora McCarthy.

5   Ibid.

ix **Anna**[2] **Conroy**, born Jul 1889 in Ohio.

x **Agnes**[2] **Conroy**, born 27 Mar 1890.

xi **Frances**[2] **Conroy**, born Mar 1892 in Ohio. She married unknown.

xii **Mark Ignatius**[2] **Conroy**, born 12 Apr 1894.

Generation 4

8. **Hermannus**[4] **Hafkenscheid**[6, 7, 8], born[9] 1 Mar 1822 in Suderwick, Westfalia (D), son of 13. Henricus Hafkenscheid and 14. Johanna Petronella Van Kronenberg. He married on 21 Feb 1846 in Sankt Michael Katholisch, Suderwick, Westfalen, Preussen 9. **Maria**

---

6   1870 US Census , PAGE 27, 17 Aug 1870. Wittemore Twp, Darlington, SC.

7   1860 US Census . "Name: Herman Hafkenschield Residence: Charleston, South Carolina Minor civil division: 6th Ward Charleston City Age: 10 years Estimated birth year: 1850 Birth place: South Carolina Gender: Male Page: 1 Family number: 2 Film number: 805216 Digital GS number: 4296156 Image number: 00450 NARA publication number: M653 Collection: 1860 United States Census". "Name: Herman Hafkenschield Residence: Charleston, South Carolina Minor civil division: 6th Ward Charleston City Age: 39 years Estimated birth year: 1821 Birth place: Holland Gender: Male Page: 1 Family number: 2 Film number: 805216 Digital GS number: 4296156 Image number: 00450 NARA publication number: M653 Collection: 1860 United States Census".

8   1880 US Census . "Other Information: Birth Year <1819> Birthplace HOLLAND Age 61 Occupation Gun Smith Marital Status M <Married> Race W <White> Head of Household C. H. HAFKENSCHIEL Relation Self Father's Birthplace HOLLAND Mother's Birthplace HOLLAND ". Family History Library Film 1254917 NA Film Number T9-0917 Page Number 87A.

9   LDS family search (Batch number C930141), C930141, call # 0865868. "01 MAR 1822 Christening: 01 MAR 1822 Sankt Michael Katholisch, Suderwick, Westfalen, Preussen". Source Information: Batch No.: Dates: Source Call No.: Type: Printout Call No.: Type: <COLSPAN=7 width="1" src="../../images/spacer.gif" height="1" IMG C930141 <search_igi.asp?batch_number=C930141&region=8> 1712 - 1877 0865868 <../../library/fhlcatalog/supermainframeset.asp?display=filmhitlist&columns=*%2C180%2C0&filmno=0865868> Film NONE <COLSPAN=7 width="1" src="../../images/spacer.gif" height="1" IMG <COLSPAN=7 width="1" src="../../images/spacer.gif" height="1" IMG Sheet: 00. Parents Named: Henricus and Johanna Petronella Van Kronenberg.

Cathrina (---) Messing, born 1822 in Holland, daughter of 15. J. Heinrich Messing and 16. Anna Van Der Linde.

Notes for Hermannus Hafkenscheid

>   Worked as Gunsmith.

Children of Hermannus Hafkenscheid and Maria Cathrina (---) Messing were as follows:

>   i   **Heinrich Wilhelm (William)**[3] **Hafkenscheil**[10], [11], born 1846. He married **Rose (---)**, born 1851 in New York, USA. Notes: Naturalized in Oct. 7,1868 in New York Court. Also called William

---

10   1880 US Census , T9-0891 Page 562. Last name spelled Hafkenscheil.

11   1860 US Census . "Name: Herman Hafkenschield Residence: Charleston, South Carolina Minor civil division: 6th Ward Charleston City Age: 10 years Estimated birth year: 1850 Birth place: South Carolina Gender: Male Page: 1 Family number: 2 Film number: 805216 Digital GS number: 4296156 Image number: 00450 NARA publication number: M653 Collection: 1860 United States Census". "Name: William Hafkenschield Residence: Charleston, South Carolina Minor civil division: 6th Ward Charleston City Age: 14 years Estimated birth year: 1846 Birth place: South Carolina Gender: Male Page: 1 Family number: 2 Film number: 805216 Digital GS number: 4296156 Image number: 00450 NARA publication number: M653 Collection: 1860 United States Census".

ii   **Herman (Harmon)[3] Hafkenscheid**[12], [13], born 1850 in South Carolina.

---

12 1861 Charleston, SC Census . "Hafkenschiel genealogy http://docsouth. unc.edu/imls/census/census.html Excerpt from Charleston, SC Census 1861 Page 62 CHURCH STREET. Runs North from South Bay, between East Bay and Meeting Street, through Ward No. 1 and partly through Ward No. 3, to Pinckney Street. Page 65 No. BRICK. WOOD. OWNERS. OCCUPANTS. 100 1 Est. Mrs. Mary Chapeau.
Daniel B. Dupont.   102
1   Mrs. Rose Casey.
Philip Boylan.   104
1   Moses D. Hyams.
H. H. Von Eitzen.   106
1   Moses D. Hyams.
Rachel Bush, f. p. c.   108
1   Est. Daniel Macauley.
Dr. J. Leslie O'Wen.   110
1   Corporation of French Calvinistic Church.
George Allison.   WARD No. 3.

112   1
Mrs. Rudulph.   Mrs. Milnor, Boarding.
114   2
Jacob Allison Lockwood.
J. A. Lockwood.   116
1   Mrs. Catharine Early.
Harman Hafkenschiel.
118   1
Mrs. Catharine Early.
James O'Neill.   120
1   Thos. L. Quackenbush.
Michael McInerny. ".
13 1860 US Census . "Name: Herman Hafkenschield Residence: Charleston, South Carolina Minor civil division: 6th Ward Charleston City Age: 10 years Estimated birth year: 1850 Birth place: South Carolina Gender: Male Page: 1 Family number: 2 Film number: 805216 Digital GS number: 4296156 Image number: 00450 NARA publication number: M653 Collection: 1860 United States Census". "Name: Herman Hafkenschield Residence: Charleston, South Carolina Minor civil division: 6th Ward Charleston City Age: 10 years Estimated birth year: 1850 Birth place: South Carolina Gender: Male Page: 1 Family number: 2 Film number: 805216 Digital GS number: 4296156 Image number: 00450 NARA publication number: M653 Collection: 1860 United States Census".

4   iii **Henry**³ **Hafkenschiel**[14], born 1851/52 in South Carolina; died 9 Sep 1892 in Cold Spring< NY. He married **Nora McCarthy**, born Dec 1855 in Ireland; died 29 Mar 1939.

iv **Marie**³ **Hafkenscheid**[15], born 1862 in South Carolina.

10. **Peter**⁴ **Conroy**, born in Ballinrobe,County Mayo, Ireland. He married unknown.

Children of Peter Conroy were as follows:
6   i   **Mark**³ **Conroy**[16], born 11 Mar 1854 in Ballinrobe,County Mayo, Ireland; died 26 Jan 1938 in Youngstown, Ohio. He married **Mary Joyce**[17], born 8 Sep 1852 in County Galway, Ireland; died 21 Apr 1922 in Youngstown, Ohio, daughter of John Joyce and Bridget Conge.

11. **John**⁴ **Joyce**[18], born Jun 1827 in Ireland; died in Maam P O, Co. Galway, Ireland. He married 12. **Bridget Conge**, born Feb 1834 in Ireland; died in Maam P O, Co. Galway, Ireland.

Children of John Joyce and Bridget Conge were as follows:
7   i **Mary**³ **Joyce**[19], born 8 Sep 1852 in County Galway, Ireland; died 21 Apr 1922 in Youngstown, Ohio. She married

---

14 Ibid., "Name: Henry Hafkenschield Residence: Charleston, South Carolina Minor civil division: 6th Ward Charleston City Age: 8 years Estimated birth year: 1852 Birth place: South Carolina Gender: Male Page: 1 Family number: 2 Film number: 805216 Digital GS number: 4296156 Image number: 00450 NARA publication number: M653 Collection: 1860 United States Census".
15 1870 US Census . "Name: Marie Hafkenscheil Estimated birth year: 1862 Gender: Female Age: 8y Race or color (expanded): White Birth place: South Carolina Residence: South Carolina, United States Collection: 1870 United States Census".
16 Ohio Deaths .
17 Ibid.
18 1900 US Census .
19 Ohio Deaths .

Mark Conroy[20], born 11 Mar 1854 in Ballinrobe,County Mayo, Ireland; died 26 Jan 1938 in Youngstown, Ohio, son of Peter Conroy.

ii   **Celia**[3] **Joyce**, born May.

Generation 5

13. **Henricus**[5] **Hafkenscheid**, born 1796, son of 17. Christian Franziscus Hafkenscheid and 18. Everdina Bouman. He married on 16 Feb 1821 in Sankt Michael Katholisch, Suderwick, Westfalen, Preussen 14. **Johanna Petronella Van Kronenberg**, christened[21] 28 Dec 1798 in Sankt Michael Katholisch, Suderwick, Westfalen, Preussen, daughter of 19. Hermanus Van Kronenberg and 20. Adelheida Ten Bensel.

Children of Henricus Hafkenscheid and Johanna Petronella Van Kronenberg were as follows:

---

20   Ibid.

21   LDS family search (Batch number C930141). "01 MAR 1822 Christening: 01 MAR 1822 Sankt Michael Katholisch, Suderwick, Westfalen, Preussen". Source Information: Batch No.: Dates: Source Call No.: Type: Printout Call No.: Type: <COLSPAN=7 width="1" src="../../ images/spacer.gif" height="1" IMG C930141 <search_igi.asp?batch_ number=C930141&region=8> 1712 - 1877 0865868 <../../library/fhlcatalog/ supermainframeset.asp?display=filmhitlist&columns=*%2C180%2C0&filmn o=0865868> Film NONE <COLSPAN=7 width="1" src="../../images/spacer. gif" height="1" IMG <COLSPAN=7 width="1" src="../../images/spacer.gif" height="1" IMG Sheet: 00. Kronenberg spelled Cronenberg in this citation.

8   i   **Hermannus**⁴ **Hafkenscheid**²², ²³, ²⁴, born²⁵ 1 Mar 1822 in Suderwick (D). He married on 21 Feb 1846 in Sankt Michael Katholisch, Suderwick, Westfalen, Preussen **Maria Cathrina (---) Messing**, born 1822 in Holland, daughter of J. Heinrich Messing and Anna Van Der Linde.

ii **Everdina**⁴ **Hafkenscheid**, born 1823.

iii **Wilhelmus**⁴ **Hafkenscheid**, born 1825.

iv **Aleida**⁴ **Hafkenscheid**, born 1827.

v **Johannes**⁴ **Hafkenscheid**, born 1829. Notes: Went to America in 1855

vi **Henrica Carolina**⁴ **Hafkenscheid**, born 1831.

vii **Christianus Franciscus**⁴ **Hafkenscheid**, born 1834.

---

22 1870 US Census , PAGE 27, 17 Aug 1870. Wittemore Twp, Darlington, SC.

23 1860 US Census . "Name: Herman Hafkenschield Residence: Charleston, South Carolina Minor civil division: 6th Ward Charleston City Age: 10 years Estimated birth year: 1850 Birth place: South Carolina Gender: Male Page: 1 Family number: 2 Film number: 805216 Digital GS number: 4296156 Image number: 00450 NARA publication number: M653 Collection: 1860 United States Census". "Name: Herman Hafkenschield Residence: Charleston, South Carolina Minor civil division: 6th Ward Charleston City Age: 39 years Estimated birth year: 1821 Birth place: Holland Gender: Male Page: 1 Family number: 2 Film number: 805216 Digital GS number: 4296156 Image number: 00450 NARA publication number: M653 Collection: 1860 United States Census".

24 1880 US Census . "Other Information: Birth Year <1819> Birthplace HOLLAND Age 61 Occupation Gun Smith Marital Status M <Married> Race W <White> Head of Household C. H. HAFKENSCHIEL Relation Self Father's Birthplace HOLLAND Mother's Birthplace HOLLAND ". Family History Library Film 1254917 NA Film Number T9-0917 Page Number 87A.

25 LDS family search (Batch number C930141), C930141, call # 0865868. "01 MAR 1822 Christening: 01 MAR 1822 Sankt Michael Katholisch, Suderwick, Westfalen, Preussen". Source Information: Batch No.: Dates: Source Call No.: Type: Printout Call No.: Type: <COLSPAN=7 width="1" src="../../images/spacer.gif" height="1" IMG C930141 <search_igi.asp?batch_number=C930141&region=8> 1712 - 1877 0865868 <../../library/fhlcatalog/supermainframeset.asp?display=filmhitlist&columns=*%2C180%2C0&filmno=0865868> Film NONE <COLSPAN=7 width="1" src="../../images/spacer.gif" height="1" IMG <COLSPAN=7 width="1" src="../../images/spacer.gif" height="1" IMG Sheet: 00. Parents Named: Henricus and Johanna Petronella Van Kronenberg.

15. J. Heinrich[5] Messing. He married 16. Anna Van Der Linde.

Children of J. Heinrich Messing and Anna Van Der Linde were as follows:

9   i   **Maria Cathrina**[4] **(---) Messing**, born 1822 in Holland. She married on 21 Feb 1846 in Sankt Michael Katholisch, Suderwick, Westfalen, Preussen **Hermannus Hafkenscheid**[26, 27, 28], born[29] 1 Mar 1822 in Suderwick (D), son of Henricus Hafkenscheid and Johanna Petronella Van Kronenberg.

---

26 1870 US Census , PAGE 27, 17 Aug 1870. Wittemore Twp, Darlington, SC.
27 1860 US Census . "Name: Herman Hafkenschield Residence: Charleston, South Carolina Minor civil division: 6th Ward Charleston City Age: 10 years Estimated birth year: 1850 Birth place: South Carolina Gender: Male Page: 1 Family number: 2 Film number: 805216 Digital GS number: 4296156 Image number: 00450 NARA publication number: M653 Collection: 1860 United States Census". "Name: Herman Hafkenschield Residence: Charleston, South Carolina Minor civil division: 6th Ward Charleston City Age: 39 years Estimated birth year: 1821 Birth place: Holland Gender: Male Page: 1 Family number: 2 Film number: 805216 Digital GS number: 4296156 Image number: 00450 NARA publication number: M653 Collection: 1860 United States Census".
28 1880 US Census . "Other Information: Birth Year <1819> Birthplace HOLLAND Age 61 Occupation Gun Smith Marital Status M <Married> Race W <White> Head of Household C. H. HAFKENSCHIEL Relation Self Father's Birthplace HOLLAND Mother's Birthplace HOLLAND ". Family History Library Film 1254917 NA Film Number T9-0917 Page Number 87A.
29 LDS family search (Batch number C930141), C930141, call # 0865868. "01 MAR 1822 Christening: 01 MAR 1822 Sankt Michael Katholisch, Suderwick, Westfalen, Preussen". Source Information: Batch No.: Dates: Source Call No.: Type: Printout Call No.: Type: <COLSPAN=7 width="1" src="../../images/spacer.gif" height="1" IMG C930141 <search_igi.asp?batch_number=C930141&region=8> 1712 - 1877 0865868 <../../library/fhlcatalog/supermainframeset.asp?display=filmhitlist&columns=*%2C180%2C0&filmno=0865868> Film NONE <COLSPAN=7 width="1" src="../../images/spacer.gif" height="1" IMG <COLSPAN=7 width="1" src="../../images/spacer.gif" height="1" IMG Sheet: 00. Parents Named: Henricus and Johanna Petronella Van Kronenberg.

Generation 6

17. Christian Franziscus⁶ **Hafkenscheid**, born 1763; died 10 Jul 1832, son of 21. Franziskus Wilhelmus Hafkenscheid and 22. Johanna Overgoor. He married on 25 Oct 1789 in Gendringen 18. **Everdina Bouman**, born 1764 in Ulft, Holland, daughter of 23. Cornelius Bouman and 24. Mechtildis Mechtelt Mommen.

<u>Notes for Christian Franziscus Hafkenscheid</u>
   Houtdrost (Wood taskmaster)

Children of Christian Franziscus Hafkenscheid and Everdina Bouman were as follows:
   13   i **Henricus**⁵ **Hafkenscheid**, born 1796. He married on 16 Feb 1821 in Sankt Michael Katholisch, Suderwick, Westfalen, Preussen **Johanna Petronella Van Kronenberg**, christened[30] 28 Dec 1798 in Sankt Michael Katholisch, Suderwick, Westfalen, Preussen, daughter of Hermanus Van Kronenberg and Adelheida Ten Bensel.
        ii **Joannes Fredericus**⁵ **Hafkenscheid**, born 1792.
        iii **Theodorus**⁵ **Hafkenscheid**, born 1794.
        iv **Franciscus Wilhelmus**⁵ **Hafkenscheid**, born 1798; died 1858.
        v **Hendrina**⁵ **Hafkenscheid**, born 1805.
        vi **Margaretha**⁵ **Hafkenscheid**, born 1805.

19. Hermanus⁶ **Van Kronenberg**, died 11 May 1802 in Dinxperlo. He married on 17 Jun 1784 in Sankt Michael Katholisch, Suderwick, Westfalen, Preussen 20. **Adelheida Ten Bensel**.

Children of Hermanus Van Kronenberg and Adelheida Ten Bensel were as follows:
   14   i **Johanna Petronella**⁵ **Van Kronenberg**, christened[31] 28 Dec 1798 in Sankt Michael Katholisch, Suderwick, Westfalen, Preussen. She married on 16 Feb 1821 in Sankt Michael Katholisch, Suderwick, Westfalen, Preussen

---

30 Ibid., Kronenberg spelled Cronenberg in this citation.
31 Ibid., Kronenberg spelled Cronenberg in this citation.

Henricus Hafkenscheid, born 1796, son of Christian Franziscus Hafkenscheid and Everdina Bouman.

ii **Joanna**[5] **Van Kronenberg**, born 1788.

iii **Theodara**[5] **Van Kronenberg**, born 1790.

iv **Johanna Wilhelmina**[5] **Van Kronenberg**, born 1792.

v **Johan Wilhelm**[5] **Van Kronenberg**, born 1794.

vi **Johannes Theodoor**[5] **Van Kronenberg**, born 1796; died 1869.

Generation 7

21. **Franziskus Wilhelmus**[7] **Hafkenscheid**, born 1 Nov 1731, son of 25. Fredericus Hafkenscheid and 26. Joanna Knippenborgh. He married 22. **Johanna Overgoor**, born abt 11 Jul 1725, daughter of 27. Jannes Overgoor and 28. Henderieckske Aalders.

Children of Franziskus Wilhelmus Hafkenscheid and Johanna Overgoor were as follows:

17   i **Christian Franziscus**[6] **Hafkenscheid**, born 1763; died 10 Jul 1832. He married on 25 Oct 1789 in Gendringen **Everdina Bouman**, born 1764 in Ulft, Holland, daughter of Cornelius Bouman and Mechtildis Mechtelt Mommen.

ii **Joanna Frederica**[6] **Hafkenscheid**, born 1757.

iii **Henrica**[6] **Hafkenscheid**, born 1759.

23. **Cornelius**[7] **Bouman**, born 1720; died 21 Dec 1783 in Megchelen, Holland, son of 29. Arnouldus Aarent Bouman and 30. Elisabeth Ratelbant. He married in 1751 in Gendringen 24. **Mechtildis Mechtelt Mommen**, born 1729 in Bislich; died 11 Feb 1814 in Megchelen, Holland.

Children of Cornelius Bouman and Mechtildis Mechtelt Mommen were as follows:

18   i **Everdina**[6] **Bouman**, born 1764 in Ulft, Holland. She married on 25 Oct 1789 in Gendringen **Christian Franziscus Hafkenscheid**, born 1763; died 10 Jul 1832,

son of Franziskus Wilhelmus Hafkenscheid and Johanna Overgoor.

Generation 8

25. Fredericus[8] **Hafkenscheid**, born 24 Aug 1700; died 9 Jul 1766, son of 31. Johannes Fredericus Hafkenscheid and 32. Theodora Borckes. He married on 30 May 1726 in Ulft, Holland 26. **Joanna Knippenborgh**, born 2 Jan 1702; died 10 Jan 1769.

Notes for Fredericus Hafkenscheid
Followed his father as Viscount 2 of the house of Ulft. After the fall of the house Ulft he started a cafe called "The Arms of Bergh."_His godfather was Servatius BOCHEIM and his godmother Christiane Gräfin Frederica von Hohenzollern-Sigmaringen.

Children of Fredericus Hafkenscheid and Joanna Knippenborgh were as follows:

    21   i   **Franziskus Wilhelmus**[7] **Hafkenscheid**, born 1 Nov 1731. He married **Johanna Overgoor**, born abt 11 Jul 1725, daughter of Jannes Overgoor and Henderieckske Aalders.

          ii   **Christianus Maximilianus**[7] **Hafkenscheid**. He married **Gesina Westervelt**, born 1740; died 25 Dec 1800.

         iii **Oswaldina Antonetta**[7] **Hafkenscheid**.

         iv **Maria Franciska**[7] **Hafkenscheid**.

         v   **Theodora**[7] **Hafkenscheid**.

         vi **Franciska**[7] **Hafkenscheid**.

27. Jannes[8] **Overgoor**. He married 28. **Henderieckske Aalders**.

Children of Jannes Overgoor and Henderieckske Aalders were as follows:

    22   i   **Johanna**[7] **Overgoor**, born abt 11 Jul 1725. She married **Franziskus Wilhelmus Hafkenscheid**, born

1 Nov 1731, son of Fredericus Hafkenscheid and Joanna Knippenborgh.

29. **Arnouldus Aarent**[8] **Bouman**, born 1690; died before 1751. He married on 23 Feb 1715 30. **Elisabeth Ratelbant**, born 1690; died 29 May 1778.

Children of Arnouldus Aarent Bouman and Elisabeth Ratelbant were as follows:

> 23   i **Cornelius**[7] **Bouman**, born 1720; died 21 Dec 1783 in Megchelen, Holland. He married in 1751 in Gendringen **Mechtildis Mechtelt Mommen**, born 1729 in Bislich; died 11 Feb 1814 in Megchelen, Holland.

Generation 9

31. **Johannes Fredericus**[9] **Hafkenscheid**, born 1660; died 11 Aug 1722. He married 32. **Theodora Borckes**, died 12 Aug 1715, daughter of 33. Dirck Borckes.

Notes for Johannes Fredericus Hafkenscheid

> Was in 1690 by the Earl of Bergh appointed as supervisor for hunting and fishing. He was Burggraf of the house of Ulft on April 2, 1691

Children of Johannes Fredericus Hafkenscheid and Theodora Borckes were as follows:

> 25   i **Fredericus**[8] **Hafkenscheid**, born 24 Aug 1700; died 9 Jul 1766. He married on 30 May 1726 in Ulft, Holland **Joanna Knippenborgh**, born 2 Jan 1702; died 10 Jan 1769.

Generation 10

33. **Dirck**[10] **Borckes**. He married unknown.

Children of Dirck Borckes were as follows:

32   i **Theodora**[9] **Borckes**, died 12 Aug 1715. She married **Johannes Fredericus Hafkenscheid**, born 1660; died 11 Aug 1722.

www.ingramcontent.com/pod-product-compliance
Lightning Source LLC
Chambersburg PA
CBHW061404280526
45784CB00001B/359